# THE LOVE STORY OF
# YEATS AND MAUD GONNE

# The Love Story of Yeats and Maud Gonne

by

## Margery Brady

MERCIER PRESS

MERCIER PRESS
PO Box 5, 5 French Church Street, Cork
16 Hume Street, Dublin 2

© M. Brady, 1990

ISBN 0 85342 935 9

*A CIP record is available for this book from the British Library.*

15  14  13  12  11  10  9  8  7  6

FOR FAMILY AND FRIENDS

### ACKNOWLEDGEMENTS

Encouragement was given by family and friends to whom this book is dedicated. Books and newspapers used for research are listed in the Bibliography but extra information was supplied by Ellen Thomas on behalf of the Rector of St Paul's Church, Tongham, by Lord Dunboyne and by Paddy MacGrath, Tipperary.

I was very appreciative of a letter from Michael B. Yeats, son of the poet, who read the first draft and sent his best wishes.

My most grateful thanks are due to Catherine Rose and all the staff of the Mercier Press for their help.

Printed in Ireland by Colour Books Ltd.

# Introduction

A local class in English literature re-introduced me to the poetry of W.B. Yeats. Long ago I had read, and half forgotten, a biography of Maud Gonne and wondered why she had not responded to the love expressed in his wonderful poems. Taking this narrow view I read everything I could lay my hands on about this fated pair and sifted out the story of his great love for her.

This is not a dissertation about Yeats' work, nor is it about the history of the day or the political involvements of Maud Gonne. It is a love story, illustrated with some of the most poignant poems ever written. I do not claim that the story is wholly complete although the facts were well researched and the sources are listed: there are many scholars who know far more than I about the subject and I would welcome any information that will add to this account. Each section is introduced with a few lines of Yeats' poetry.

The writings of W.B. Yeats are vast and provide an accurate record of his thoughts. Maud Gonne's autobiography, in contrast, is a romantic version of what she remembered, or wished to remember, when she wrote it as an old woman in her seventies. Even at that age, she did not admit her relationship with her own daughter, Iseult. The interview she gave to the *New York Evening World* in August 1905 gives, more honestly, her views on marriage, at least, when she was a younger woman.

A.N. Jeffares and Joseph Hone concentrate more on Yeats' literary achievements than his love life, while Maud's biographers, Samuel Levenson and Nancy Cardozo give far more details about her romantic involvement with Yeats. The chronology of events in their lives is different in most books. Dates of particular occasions differ; for example, there are at least three different dates given for the birth of Maud's first child, and two different sexes. I have attempted here to set down, in date sequence, all the details I thought relevant and then to weave them into a story.

Some questions about W.B. Yeats and Maud Gonne's relationship are answered, but many are not. Was Maud worthy of such beautiful poems? Would Yeats have written so well if she had married him or even returned his love? Was it only in the agony of unrequited pursuit that he could write and would the ecstasy of fulfilment have been short-lived or uninspiring? He admits that, because of her, he wrote much of his best work; she was to say that the world would one day thank her for not marrying him since he made poetry out of his 'unhappiness'.

Fitting the facts together was interesting but finding new information was exciting. For instance Maud's birth was never registered so I sent to Tongham Church for a copy of her baptismal certificate. This source also revealed the birth of a second sister of Maud's Margaretta Rose. Similarly, Yeats had a passion to find out about his ancestors and could not trace the Countess of Ossory who, he believed, contacted him. With great delight and the help of Lord Dunboyne I discovered the details that eluded him thus providing another link to Kilkenny where I live.

Writing this book transformed Maud Gonne and Willie Yeats from vague literary figures into understandable real people. This brought an understanding of his love poems, thus coming full circle to my first quest.

# Main Characters

*Butler, Mary*: Married Benjamin Yeats, grandson of Jervis Yeats. From the time of the marriage the name of Butler was added to that of Yeats. Direct descendant of the third Earl of Ormond. Brought income to the family from land in Ireland.

*Cook, Edith*: Maud's mother. From wealthy commercial/industrial English family. Orphaned early in life. Died age 27.

*Cook, Emily Lucas*: Maud's godmother. First wife of Sir Francis, Maud's grand uncle. Francis bought Monserrate near Lisbon for her. She suggested to Tommy Gonne that his daughters should be educated in France.

*Cook, Sir Francis*: Maud's grand uncle with whom Maud lived for a time when her mother died. Created a baronet in 1888 for support of the arts.

*Cook, William*: (1784–1869) Came from a farm in Norfolk to make fortune in linen/drapery business. Died leaving £2,000,000.

*de la Sizeranne, Comtesse*: (Aunt Mary) Maud's twice married paternal grand aunt who longed to launch Maud in Paris. She took Maud to Royat where she met Lucien Millevoye.

*Gonne, (Edith) Maud*: (1866–1953) Irish Nationalist and one of the great beauties of her age. Remembered not so much for her political work but because she was immortalised in poetry.

*Gonne, Iseult*: (1894–1954) Daughter of Maud and Lucien Millevoye. Married the poet Francis Stuart in 1920. Outlived her mother by a year.

*Gonne, Thomas*: (1835–1886) Maud's adored father. Second son of a wine importer. Served with distinction in the British army in India. Late convert to Irish Nationalism.

*Gonne, William*: Maud's paternal uncle and her guardian when her father died in 1886. Wine importer. Very strict with Maud and told her, incorrectly, that her inheritance was minimal.

*Gregory, Lady Augusta*: Author, landowner, widow whose home at Coole Park became a meeting place for the literary figures of the day. Patron, nurse, surrogate mother to W.B. Yeats.

*Hyde-Lees, George*: Married W.B. Yeats in 1917. Mother of Anne and Michael. Related through marriage to Olivia Shakespear. Well-educated, a linguist with an interest in the arts.

*MacBride, John*: Married Maud in 1903. Father of Seán. An assayer, he was an Irish Nationalist who fought valiantly against the British in the Boer War.

*MacBride, Seán*: Son of Maud and John MacBride. Reared in France until 1916. In his later years he was awarded the Nobel Peace Prize.

*Millevoye, Lucien*: The love of Maud's life and father of Georgette and Iseult Gonne. Journalist, magistrate with great interest in politics. Married but estranged from his wife Adrienne. He had one son Henri Millevoye.

*O'Leary, Ellen*: Sister of Nationalist John O'Leary. Poet. Gave Maud letter of introduction to J.B. and W.B. Yeats.

*O'Leary, John*: Irish Nationalist who encouraged W.B. Yeats to become one of Ireland's leading poets and interested Maud in W.B.'s poetry to divert her from her more militant form of Nationalism.

*Pollexfen, Susan*: Wife of J.B. Yeats and mother of W.B. Prettiest sister of George Pollexfen her husband's best friend. Belonged to wealthy merchant family in Sligo.

*Pollexfen, William*: W.B.'s maternal grandfather. Ran away to sea. Returned and married Elizabeth Middleton and became partner, with her brother, in milling and shipping companies in Sligo.

*Quinn, John*: Wealthy American lawyer, son of Irish imigrants. Came to know the group through notes Lady Gregory wrote about Jack Yeats' paintings. Thereafter became great friend of Yeats' group and patron of the Irish arts.

*Shakespear, Olivia*: W.B.'s first lover. Author. Married unhappily to a solicitor. Related through marriage to George Hyde-Lees.

*Yeats, Jervis*: Came to Ireland from Yorkshire. Successful linen merchant. Died 1712.

*Yeats, John Butler*: Son of Mary Butler Yeats and great-grandfather of W.B. Clergyman (Parson Yeats) who first brought the Yeats family to Drumcliffe in Sligo.

*Yeats, John Butler (J.B.)*:(1839–1922) Father of W.B. Artist, author/philosopher. Qualified but never practised as barrister. Formative influence on his family.

*Yeats William Butler: (Willie or W.B.)*: (1865–1939) Poet whose lifelong love for Maud Gonne inspired his most poignant poems.

*Yeats William Butler*: (1806–1862) Rector. Grandfather of W.B. Married Jane Corbet.

# 1

*Tall and noble but with face and bosom*
*Delicate in colour as apple blossom . . .*

THE ARROW

On 30 January 1889, a hansom cab drove along a quiet, tree-lined street in London's suburb of Chiswick. It stopped outside Number 3, Blenheim Road, the home of the Yeats family. Its passenger, a striking 22 year-old woman who had come from Belgravia, asked the driver to wait. She had red-gold hair and hazel eyes, and was said to be 'well dressed in a careless fashion'. Maud Gonne had come to call on John Butler (J.B.) Yeats and his son, Willie (W.B.). She had a letter of introduction from Ellen O' Leary, sister of John, the well-known Irish Nationalist. Ellen had written to Willie, 'I gave Miss Gonne, a new lady friend of ours and new convert to love of Ireland, a letter of introduction to your father. I'm sure she and you will like each other. An artist and a poet could not fail to admire her. She is so charming, fine and handsome. Most of our male friends admire her.'

All the Yeatses assembled in the sitting room to welcome Maud — all except Mrs Yeats who had recently suffered a stroke. J.B., the father and very much the dominant member of the family, had high aesthetic ideals but little money; he earned a precarious living from portrait-painting. Willie, his son, then aged 23, had just published *The Wanderings of Oisín and other poems* with the help of John O'Leary. His brother Jack, then 16, was to follow in his father's footsteps as an artist.

Willie's two sisters were particularly intrigued with this interesting visitor who had abandoned a social life in the viceregal court for Irish Nationalism. Susan Mary, known as Lily, worked as an embroideress under May

Morris. She was to note that Maud wore slippers at this first meeting. Her sister, Elizabeth (nicknamed Lolly) was a student mistress at Chiswick High School. According to Samuel Levenson she recorded her impressions in her diary that evening: 'Miss Gonne, the Dublin beauty (who is marching on to glory over the hearts of the Dublin youths), called today on Willie, of course, but also apparently on Papa. She is immensely tall and very stylish . . . she has a rich complexion and hazel eyes and is, I think, decidedly handsome.'

Turning away from the rest of the family, Maud gave her attention to J.B. and Willie. She talked to both men about Irish problems — Ireland, dominated by its neighbour for six hundred years, was once more fighting for its rights. Political prisoners had been taken but the power of the British landowners was being eroded by the Land League. Maud's Nationalism had taken a militant form and she felt that, in a political struggle, the end justified the means, even if these means were violent.

J.B. was totally opposed to violence, but Willie was so smitten by her great beauty that he was slow to disagree with her. In an effort to steer her towards Ireland's cultural aspirations, John O'Leary had given Maud a copy of Willie's recently published poetry. She now turned to him and declared she had cried over certain passages.

From first sight, Willie was in love with Maud — 'the troubling of my life began.' Of this first meeting he wrote in *Memoirs of W.B. Yeats*: 'I had never thought to see in a living woman so great beauty. It belonged to famous pictures, to poetry, to some legendary past. A complexion like the blossoms of apples, and yet face and body had the beauty of lineaments which Blake calls the highest beauty because it changes least from youth to age, and a stature so great that she seemed of a divine race . . . she brought into my life . . . a sound as of a Burmese gong, an overpowering tumult that had yet many pleasant secondary notes.'

He wrote a poem — *The Arrow* — to honour this first meeting:

> *I thought of your beauty, and this arrow,*
> *Made out of a wild thought, is in my marrow.*
> *There's no man may look upon her, no man,*
> *As when newly grown to be a woman,*
> *Tall and noble but with face and bosom*
> *Delicate in colour as apple blossom.*
> *This beauty's kinder, yet for a reason*
> *I could weep that the old is out of season.*

The Yeats family had heard of Maud's great beauty, yet her name was not linked with any of the men around Dublin. Katherine Tynan, a friend of the family, had told them that all her male friends, young and old, were in love with Maud, but 'they soon got over it. . . . Her aloofness must have chilled the most ardent lover.' Katherine described Willie at this time too — 'all dreams and gentleness . . . beautiful to look at with his dark face, its touch of vivid colouring, the night black hair, the eager eyes . . . he lived, breathed, ate drank and slept poetry.'

Maud recalls a rather different picture. She is said to have remembered 'A tall lanky boy with deep-set eyes behind glasses, over which a lock of dark hair was constantly falling, often stained with paint — dressed in shabby clothes . . .'

However, before she left, Maud invited Willie to visit her later that day in her rooms at Ebury Street in Belgravia. There he dined with Maud, her sister Kathleen and a cousin. On that occasion, he thought Maud clever as well as beautiful; he was, however, wary of her 'sensational' views on European politics.

11

Two days after this visit, he wrote to Ellen O'Leary: 'Did I tell you how much I admire Miss Gonne? She will make many conversions to her political belief. If she said the world was flat and the moon an old caubeen tossed up into the sky I would be proud to be of her party.'

# 2

*Before us lies eternity; our souls*
*Are love, and a continual farewell.*

A common interest in Ireland had brought Willie and
Maud together. Their backgrounds show they had much
more in common — both were of English stock and had an
interest in the linen trade. The Yeatses, who came from
Yorkshire to Dublin in the seventeenth century, had been
linen merchants for three generations. Maud's mother,
Edith Cook, came from a family with origins in Norfolk
who had built up a considerable fortune in the linen and
drapery business also. From the merchant classes, too,
Willie's mother's family of Pollexfens and Middletons
were well-known shipbuilders and millers in Sligo in the
west of Ireland while Maud's father's family were successful wine importers in London.

Both commercially-minded families helped with the
rearing of Willie and Maud but in each case it was the
father who broke with family tradition and became the
major influence in the family.

Willie was obsessed with his ancestors and wrote about
them in his poetry. When one of the third generation of
linen merchants, Benjamin Yeats, married Mary Butler, the
family acquired 560 acres of land in Thomastown which
brought in a steady income, a pension from the British war
office through her father and a beautiful silver drinking cup
dated 1534 from the Ormond family. Mary was a direct
descendant of the third Earl of Ormond and Benjamin Yeats
and his descendants were pleased to include Butler in the
family name from the time of his marriage.

Mary and Benjamin had a son John born in 1774, who,
because of the additional income, enrolled at Trinity
College, Dublin and became Rector of Drumcliffe in

County Sligo in 1805. John's son William also went to Trinity College and entered the Church of Ireland so it was assumed that his son John (J.B.) who was Willie's father, would follow in the family footsteps. J.B. showed no interest in the Church and studied law instead.

Willie's grandfather, William, retired from Sligo to Dublin — to be near his brother-in-law, Robert Corbet, who lived in Sandymount Castle. One day in 1862 William, who had gone to visit Robert, died quite suddenly. Thus J.B. who was not yet qualified, inherited the estate in Kildare.

A year after his father's death J.B. married Susan Pollexfen, sister of his good friend George, at St John's Church in Sligo. Years later J.B. said of his son's talent that his lyrical gift was Yeats but his poetical heredity was Pollexfen: 'By marriage with the Pollexfens I have given a tongue to the sea cliffs.' William Butler Yeats their first child, was born at 'Georgeville', now 5, Sandymount Avenue, Dublin, late at night on 13 June 1865.

Little is known about the Gonnes but Maud maintained they had some Irish blood. The Cooks could be traced back to 1805 when William Cook left a sheep farm in Norfolk to work in a linen store in London. After a meteoric rise in the wholesale side of the business he died at the ripe old age of eighty-five, leaving a £2 million fortune to his two sons and three daughters. His eldest son, also William, was Maud's grandfather. Both Maud's grandparents died young leaving two daughters Edith and Emma, to be reared by aunts and Uncle Frank or Francis. Francis was by far the most flamboyant member of the family. He collected paintings and, for his support of the arts, was created a baronet in 1888. He married twice, first to Emily Lucas in Lisbon and secondly to an American divorcee Tennessee Celeste Claflin.

Sir Francis became one of Edith Frith Cook's guardians and held her inheritance in trust until, at twenty-one, she married thirty year old Thomas Gonne on 19 December

1865 at East Peckham in Kent. Tommy, as he was called, was a second son and, as he would not inherit the family business, bought a commission in the British army and was decorated for service in India.

Tommy and Edith had three daughters — Maud was the eldest — yet none of the births was registered which led to speculation about Maud's date of birth. As the family first lived in Tongham in Surrey I wrote to the parish church and received a copy of Maud's baptismal certificate. This shows that Edith Maud Gonne, daughter of Thomas and Edith Frith Gonne was baptised by William Dyer on 21 January 1867. As it was the custom to baptise children approximately one month after birth it would suggest that Maud was born around the 21 December 1866, nearly a year after her parents' marriage.

Willie and Maud, born eighteen months apart, would both live nomadic childhoods dominated by their fathers while neither mother enjoyed good health.

## Family Tree of W.B. Yeats (limited to those mentioned in book)

Jervis Yeats from Yorkshire (d.1712)

Benjamin Yeats

Benjamin Yeats m. Mary Butler
Descendant of 1st 2nd and 3rd Earls of Ormond

John Butler Yeats (b.1774)
m. Jane Taylor (1803)

William Butler Yeats (1806-62) — Thomas Butler Yeats

John Butler Yeats (1839-1922)
m. Jane Corbet (1836)

? Pollexfen — Torquay
m. Mary Stephens — Wexford

William Pollexfen
m. Elizabeth Middleton

Charles Pollexfen (1838-1927) — George Pollexfen (1839-1910) — Susan Pollexfen (d.1900)

m. (1863)

Children of John Butler Yeats and Susan Pollexfen:

- William (Willie) Butler Yeats (1865-1939)
- Susan Mary (Lily) Butler Yeats (b.1866)
- Elizabeth (Lolly) Butler Yeats (b.1868)
- Robert (Bobbie) Butler Yeats (1870-73)
- John (Jack) Butler Yeats (1871-1957)
- Jane Grace Butler Yeats (b. & d.1875)

m. George Hyde Lees (1917)

- Anne Butler Yeats (b.1919)
- Michael Butler Yeats (b.1921)

## Family of Maud Gonne (confined to those mentioned in book)

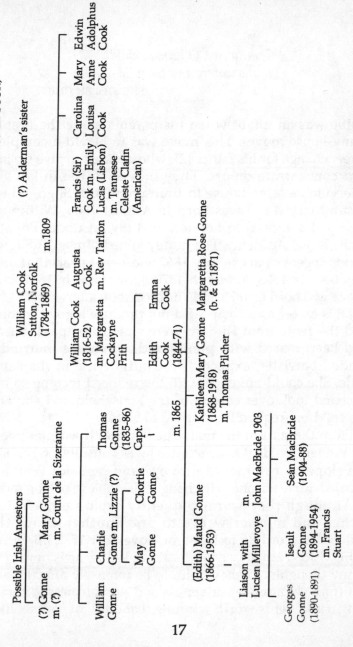

# 3

*Come away, O human child!*
*To the waters and the wild* . . .
THE STOLEN CHILD

Willie was an infant when his parents made the first of
many house moves. This move was to herald a complete
career change for his father J.B. who decided to give up law
and concentrate on art. They moved to the in-laws at
'Merville', a large house in Enniscrone, Co. Sligo, where
Susan Mary (Lily) was born in August 1866. Within six
months J.B. moved to London to study art under Poynter
at the Royal Academy. The family joined him at 23 Fitzroy
Road, Regent's Park in July 1867 and here Elizabeth (Lolly)
was born in 1868, Robert in 1870, John (Jack) in 1871. Jane
Grace was born in 1875 and she died soon afterwards.

J.B.'s career as an artist did not produce a good income
and the rents from Kildare were slow to be paid. Susan
had been reared with plenty and, when she married a
landed barrister, expected to continue life in the same
style. She could not cope with the reduced income so her
husband took over control of the household and she and
the children frequently returned to Sligo.

From the start of the marriage her health was not good.
Sir William Wilde (Oscar's father) was consulted when she
developed a cataract in one eye and he said: 'You are
married, leave it alone.' He changed the topic to fishing rods!

Although they were frequently separated, Willie's
father and mother wrote to one another about the
children. According to Hone in November 1872 J.B. wrote
to his wife: 'I am very anxious about Willie, he is never out
of my thoughts. I believe him to be intensely affectionate,
but from shyness, sensitiveness and nervousness, difficult
to win and yet is worth winning. I should, of course, like

to see him do what is right, but he will only develop by kindness and affection and gentleness . . .'

Occasionally Susan wrote to J.B. of her pleasure in the children and in the beautiful scenery around Sligo — 'Merville' commanded splendid views of Ben Bulben and Knocknarea — however, Willie wrote in his biography that his mother made little impression on his youth.

In Sligo the Yeats children were surrounded by relatives — the Pollexfens and Middletons, and children and grandchildren of Parson Yeats of Drumcliffe. Grandfather William Pollexfen made the most impression on Willie and, in *Reveries over Childhood and Youth* Willie wrote: 'I confused my grandfather with God . . . Even today when I read *King Lear*, his image is always before me and I wonder if the delight in passionate men in my plays and in my poetry is more than his memory.'

The Middletons mixed with the local people and it was they gave Willie his first interest in country stories. In the cottages of Rosses and Ballisodare he heard his first fairy stories, echoed in his poem *The Stolen Child*:

> *Where the wave of moonlight glosses*
> *The dim grey sands with light,*
> *Far off by furthest Rosses*
> *We foot it all the night,*
> *Weaving olden dances,*
> *Mingling hands and mingling glances*
> *Till the moon has taken flight;*
> *To and fro we leap*
> *And chase the frothy bubbles,*
> *While the world is full of troubles*
> *And is anxious in its sleep.*
> *Come away, O human child!*
> *To the waters and the wild*
> *With a faery, hand in hand,*
> *For the world's more full of weeping than you can*
>    *understand . . .*

Maud's childhood was surprisingly similar to Willie's. Shortly after her birth her father, Captain Gonne, was transferred to the Curragh in Country Kildare, England's largest military base in Ireland. His transfer was due to a massive reinforcement of the existing garrison to prevent a new Fenian rebellion.

Just as Willie and his mother crossed the Irish sea to join his father, Maud and her mother crossed in the opposite direction to join her father. Early in the spring of 1867 Maud's family settled at 'Floraville' in Dublin's Donnybrook, where a second daughter, Kathleen Mary, was born in 1868. Maud's first friend Ida lived next door at 'Airfield', home of the whiskey distiller Jameson. Just like Willie Yeats in his youth, the children heard tales of ghosts and fairies from the servant girls.

Maud's mother Edith did not enjoy good health. She was pregnant and ill with tuberculosis in the summer of 1871 and was advised to travel to the sunshine of Italy. On the journey her health deteriorated and, following the birth of a daughter, she died at Paddington in Middlesex on 21 June. She was buried four days later at the same parish church in which Maud was baptised. Her baby daughter, Margaretta Rose, died just six weeks later and shared her mother's grave.

After his wife's death, the devoted father, Tommy, returned with his daughters to Donnybrook, but soon moved to a cottage in Kildare. It was here that Maud's lifelong love of animals and birds began.

A year later Maud had a severe bronchial attack and the family moved again — this time to the sea air of Howth, in Dublin. Maud loved life here and her nurse brought the children to meet the locals who told them tales of the heroes of the 1798 Rising. The seeds of these stories were to lie dormant in Maud's mind for many years before they would flower into the Nationalism of her adult life.

Within a few years Willie Yeats, too, would roam the hills of Howth, but Maud had already left.

# 4

*The children learn to cipher and to sing,*
*To study reading-books and history* . . .

AMONG SCHOOL CHILDREN

Willie's early education began with his maternal aunts in Sligo. They found him difficult to teach and he was sent to a Dame school (a school for children run by a woman) in Sligo town. He was found to be tone deaf.

One night in 1873 his mother and a servant heard the Banshee crying and the following day his brother Robert died of croup. This was Willie's first encounter with death. To denote sympathy the ships in the harbour flew flags at half-mast and Lily and Willie drew pictures of the ships.

Soon afterwards his father decided to attend to Willie's education. J.B. read aloud to him from Macaulay and Scott. However, J.B. had little patience and shouted at Willie and, at times, threw books at him.

The Yeats family moved back to London — first to Fitzroy Road and later to Edith Villas. Between the ages of ten and fifteen Willie attended the Godolphin Day School at Hammersmith which he remembered for the ways in which boys were bullied. One year he came nineteenth out of a class of 31 in English but was very poor at spelling — a failing that persisted throughout his life.

By 1880 all rents from J.B.'s Kildare estate ceased because Irish tenants refused to pay rent to absentee landlords. The family was forced to return to Ireland where a friend loaned them a cottage in Howth. Each morning J.B. and Willie travelled into Dublin together — J.B. to his studio while his son attended a High School in Harcourt Street. In his free time Willie climbed the hills of Howth in search of insects and wild flowers. In *What Then?* he wrote:

21

*His chosen comrades thought at school*
*He must grow a famous man;*
*He thought the same and lived by rule,*
*All his twenties crammed with toil;*
*'What then?' sang Plato's ghost. 'What then?'* . . .

Just as his father found Willie hard to teach as a child, Maud's father, Tommy, found that his lively young daughters were difficult to control after their mother's death. When Maud was six he sent to England for a governess to help their nurse, Mary Anne Meredith. This was not successful so, like Willie, they were sent to live with their mother's Aunt Augusta in Hyde Park Gardens in the centre of London. This elderly lady, with the help of the nurse and governess, could ensure that the children developed good social behaviour but she had no idea how to cope with two lively little girls.

Life for them was confined and boring and soon they were sent on to live with Aunt Augusta's brother, Sir Francis Cook. His Portuguese wife, Emily, was more understanding and bought them little presents. She saw that the girls were making no progress with the governess and Maud had another attack of bronchitis. Emily advised Tommy, who was being transferred back to India, that it would be better to have the girls educated in Europe.

Tommy rented a cottage near Cannes, in the south of France where he brought his daughters and Mary Anne Meredith.The French woman he hired as governess gave them their only formal education.

*The children learn to cipher and to sing,*
*To study reading-books and history,*
*To cut and sew, be neat in everything*
*In the best modern way* . . .

Maud was ten when she left London. She spent the next five years moving through France, Italy and Switzerland, unable to put down roots and became independent. Although she was devoted to her sister, she did not form any friendships with children of her own age.

# 5

*The years to come seemed waste of breath,*
*A waste of breath the years behind*
*In balance with this life, this death.*

AN IRISH AIRMAN FORESEES HIS DEATH

Willie was so family bound it was small wonder that a distant cousin, red-haired Laura Armstrong, caught his attention. Willie was seventeen and she was three years older and already engaged. He called her Vivien and wrote a verse play, *Vivien and Time*, in which she played the title role in a house in Howth. Although she and Willie exchanged letters she married her fiance two years later.

In 1882, the year of Willie's romance, Maud's father Tommy returned from India and was delighted to find his elder daughter had grown up to be a beauty. She was pleased with his promotion to the rank of Colonel. There had always been a bond between the two and now he took her to the theatre and musical performances and also on his travels.

Kathleen was too young for these excursions, so it was only Maud who accompanied her father to Paris where they visited his Aunt Mary, the Comtesse de la Sizeranne, at her flat in the Place Vendome. Tommy, fearful of the lifestyle in Paris, would allow Maud only one day to visit the shops and drive with Great Aunt Mary in her carriage through the Bois de Boulogne.

Tommy was recalled to Ireland later in the year but the girls continued their education in Italy. On one occasion Maud managed to elude her chaperone to meet a young Italian in the Colosseum by moonlight. He proposed to her and she accepted him. When news of this reached her father, she was immediately called back to Dublin and the engagement broken off.

She was not unduly perturbed. At the time an American

was painting her portrait and she wrote in her autobiography: 'The American artist brought me a wonderful armful of flowers to the station and the Italian a large bag of chocolates which the heat had rendered sticky. I regretted the American had not been in the Colosseum, but . . . I afterwards learned he had a wife in America.'

When Maud returned to Dublin events were taking place which held no interest for her at the time but were destined to have an important bearing on her future life. Michael Davitt, a Fenian leader, had founded the Land League which was supported politically by Charles Stewart Parnell. It organised poor Irish tenants into action against eviction by Anglo-Irish landlords. Both Davitt and Parnell, together with John Dillon, had been jailed in 1881 but the British Prime Minister, Gladstone, released them the following year under the Kilmainham Treaty. The Unionists were opposed to the release of the Fenians and the viceroy and his secretary resigned in protest.

Maud and Kathleen were in Dublin on 6 May, 1882 to see the arrival of the new viceroy, Earl Spencer and his secretary Lord Frederick Cavendish but it was their father who held their attention in the parade. That night Lord Cavendish and his under-secretary, T.H. Burke were murdered in the Phoenix Park, Dublin by the Invincibles, a group of Fenians. At fifteen years of age Maud could not grasp the political implications of the times and besides the social whirl of Dublin Castle kept all knowledge of the poverty of the Irish peasants from her.

By 1885 Maud was formally launched at a series of parties. She was presented at the Viceregal Lodge and wrote in her autobiography: 'My presentation dress, embroidered with iridescent beads, looked like a fountain.'

On the following day, 17 March, she danced with the Duke of Clarence, who trod on her toes. She was rescued by his ageing father, Edwards Prince of Wales. Later while visiting her Aunt Mary in Hamburg, the Prince of Wales stopped to speak to her. Tommy, fearful that a relationship might develop and knowing that a royal invitation could not be declined, took his daughter to Bayreuth to hear Wagner's work performed in his own opera house.

Maud continued to act as her father's hostess at all social occasions at home and as his companion when he travelled abroad. Hunt balls were frequently held around Ireland and an invitation arrived to such a function in the midlands. Her father was unable to accompany her so Maud went alone. As they dined her host remarked that the Land League was ruining the country. He had evicted some of his tenants and had found them sheltering in a ditch. The wife looked poorly and would be dead before the morning. Horrified Maud asked what would be done about this and, according to her autobiography, her host replied: 'Let her die, these people must be taught a lesson.' This was the first time Maud realised that the Irish peasants, who could not or would not pay rent to their landlords, were being evicted from their homes and left to starve or emigrate. Those who took a stand were imprisoned.

Maud's beloved father Tommy also became a convert to the plight of the Irish peasants. As he and Maud watched a Land League demonstration he told her that he intended to resign his commission and to stand for parliament as a Home Rule candidate. Unfortunately this was not to be. He developed typhoid and died suddenly on 30 November 1886 in the Royal Barracks in Dublin. Tongham (Surrey) parish records show that he was 51 years old when he died and he was buried there in the family grave on 4 December 1886. Maud never ceased to grieve for his loss.

Years later Willie would write a poem, *An Irish Airman Foresees his Death*, about the death of Lady Gregory's son which would sum up Maud's feelings of that time:

> *The years to come seemed waste of breath,*
> *A waste of breath the years behind*
> *In balance with this life, this death.*

# 6

*I will find out where she has gone,*
*And kiss her lips and take her hands . . .*
THE SONG OF THE WANDERING AENGUS

Willie's new interest in poetry pleased his father. There was no money for a university education so Willie enrolled at the Metropolitan School of Art in Kildare Street where his best friend was George Russell (AE). The two wrote poetry in friendly rivalry.

Once more the Yeats family moved house — this time to 10 Ashfield Terrace in Harold's Cross, Dublin. J.B. knew many members of the Bar from his college days and hoped that they or other college celebrities, who would be more accessible at the new address, might wish to have their portraits painted. His highest ambition of the time was to 'get a judge'! He had to have a good relationship with his subject before he did a portrait and then spent many hours talking rather than painting — hence he made little money from his commissions.

Willie met many of his father's friends and was introduced to the Contemporary Club, founded by Charles Hubert Oldham (editor of the *Dublin University Review*) to discuss social, political and literary matters. Political action was barred. Here Willie read from his work and some members recognised he would soon be one of Ireland's great poets.

Among the members he met was the Fenian, John O'Leary, who had been imprisoned in Dorset's Portland Jail for Nationalist activities. John was not over anxious to talk about his jail experiences. It was his sister Ellen who told Willie about his arrest and sentence, and the Fenian movement to which he belonged. Willie found her account moving and it left him with a lasting interest in Irish Nationalism.

Meanwhile he continued his literary friendship with AE and later with the writer Katherine Tynan, whom he met in the summer of 1885. He was to see much of her at the O'Leary home and their families became lifelong friends.

Through his father Willie got to know Edward Dowden, Professor of English at Trinity College. He invited J.B. and his son to visit his book-lined house in Rathgar. Willie had been given AP Sinnett's book on *Esoteric Buddhism* by his aunt, Isabella Pollexfen, and he brought it along to Dowden's for discussion. He also showed it to his schoolfriend Charles Johnston, who became a convert to Buddhism. Charles and Willie and five other close friends founded the Dublin Hermetic Society in York Street, to promote oriental religions and magic. They claimed to have visions and power over natural forces and their beliefs were to have a profound effect on Willie's later life.

J.B. moved the family, which now included a maid called Rose and a cat called 'Daniel O'Connell', back to London in 1887. This time they lived in Earl's Court and then moved again to 3 Blenheim Road in Chiswick.

Each of the children was gainfully employed — Willie with his poetry, Jack with his drawings which were accepted by a newspaper called *The Vegetarian*. Later he invented a cartoon horse called *Signor MacCoy* for another Harmsworth publication. Lily was paid the weekly sum of ten shillings as an embroideress, working for May Morris, and was rewarded, later, by promotion as assistant to her employer. Lolly continued to teach at Chiswick School.

Although aesthetically the family seemed to be successful they had financial difficulties. The constant house moving was due to a shortage of money and J.B.'s conviction that he could do better elsewhere.

At a local club J.B. met an old friend from Trinity, John Todhunter. When he and his wife called to the Yeates Willie had to borrow three shillings from the visitors to buy tea, sugar, butter and marmalade before he could offer them refreshments.

Because J.B.'s wife, Susan, saw art as the cause of the family poverty, she took no interest in his work and neither visited his studio nor his exhibitions. Her eye cataract continued to plague her. In the summer of 1887, she suffered a paralytic stroke which affected her mind. Lily took her to an aunt in Yorkshire where she seemed to improve. Shortly after her return to London, she had a second stroke and fell downstairs. Soon she lived in just one room. Willie described her as freed 'at last from financial worry, having found perfect happiness feeding the birds at a London window.' This was why the family was without their mother when they gathered to meet Maud Gonne that January day in 1889.

Willie had a premonition that he had met Maud before — possibly because he saw her photograph at the Contemporary Club. His poem *The Song of Wandering Aengus* could have been written about this premonition:

> I went out to the hazel wood,
> Because a fire was in my head,
> And cut and peeled a hazel wand,
> And hooked a berry to a thread;
> And when white moths were on the wing,
> And moth-like stars were flickering out,
> I dropped the berry in a stream
> And caught a little silver trout.
>
> When I had laid it on the floor
> I went to blow the fire aflame,
> But something rustled on the floor,
> And someone called me by my name:
> It had become a glimmering girl
> With apple blossom in her hair
> Who called me by my name and ran

*And faded through the brightening air.*

*Though I am old with wandering*
*Through hollow lands and hilly lands,*
*I will find out where she has gone,*
*And kiss her lips and take her hands;*
*And walk among long dappled grass,*
*And pluck till time and times are done*
*The silver apples of the moon,*
*The golden apples of the sun.*

# 7

*Why, what could she have done, being what she is?*
*Was there another Troy for her to burn?*

NO SECOND TROY

After Tommy's death Maud and her sister Kathleen went
to live with Tommy's elder brother, William, the wine
importer, who had been appointed their guardian. He
lived at 11, St Helen's Place, London, and early in 1887
Maud was trying to adjust to life here after the gay life she
had led as Tommy's companion. Although more than half
of her life had been spent outside it, she felt Dublin was
her home. Willie moved back to London that same year.
He too, had spent much of his life outside of Ireland and
both felt exiled in London.

In January a Mrs Robbins called to St Helen's Place
claiming that she had a newly born baby girl who was
Tommy Gonne's child. Uncle William did not want to
believe her but Maud remembered that, as Tommy lay
dying, he had made out a cheque to someone of this name
and she accepted the story. Uncle William was persuaded
to give Mrs Robbins some money and Maud asked for her
address.

This woman was, in fact Margaret Wilson, a girl of Irish
extraction and her baby's name was Eileen. Maud visited
them at their flat on the Edgware Road and, although she
had little money when they first met she helped Margaret
and little Eileen for the following six years and then she
made more permanent arrangements for both. Margaret
Wilson had a son by an early marriage. He went to sea
and died later on in the Great War.

The reason Maud had no money to help Margaret
Wilson was because Uncle William told her and Kathleen,
incorrectly, that their father's estate was not worth much

in an attempt to restrain the girls. He said they should consider Aunt Augusta Cook's offer to adopt them.

The girls had become friendly with their cousins, May and Chortie, daughters of Charles Gonne. The four girls discussed the offer and decided they would earn their own living. Kathleen and Chortie would study art while May and Maud applied to Charing Cross Nursing Institute to become trainee nurses. May was successful but Maud was not accepted because of her weak lungs.

As a child Maud had taken elocution lessons, had acted in amateur theatricals and had been complimented by an actor of the day, Herman Vezin. He was at the Strand in London that spring, and Maud asked him to help her to become an actress. Uncle William and the family were horrified when she announced that she would make her acting debut in a repertory company as a leading lady in a play called *Heartsease*. Just before the play was to open Maud collapsed with a lung haemorrhage.

Great Aunt Mary, Countess de la Sizeranne, came to the rescue. Now living in Chelsea, she nursed Maud back to health and when she had sufficiently recovered, made arrangements for Maud and Kathleen to go to a fashionable spa at Royat in the Auvergne Mountains of central France.

While regaining her health Maud was introduced to Lucien Millevoye, a lawyer and journalist who had gone to Royat for the curative springs and also to be near his political idol General George Boulanger. Lucien was fifteen years older than Maud and was married with a son called Henri but had recently separated from his wife Adrienne.

Having met on the promenade Maud and Lucien took daily walks together and he explained that General Boulanger had lost his position as minister for war and Lucien and others were working to restore him to power. He would help France regain Alsace and Lorraine, lost to

Germany in 1870. Maud told him about the political situation in Ireland and he persuaded her to give up acting and to devote her life to becoming Ireland's Joan of Arc. England was their common enemy and they formed an alliance — he would publicise Ireland's cause in the French press and she would support the Boulangist cause. He introduced her to the General and his mistress, Marguerite Bonnemain in a country inn.

When Maud had recovered her strength, she and Lucien visited the foothills of the Puy de Dome. She could see in him qualities she had always admired in her father — he was a man of the world, mature, dashing, ready to fight for his ideals. She was extremely beautiful and he needed her consolation after the break-up of his marriage.

> *What could have made her peaceful with a mind*
> *That nobleness made simple as a fire,*
> *With beauty like a tightened bow, a kind*
> *That is not natural in a age like this,*
> *Being high and solitary and most stern?*
> *Why, what could she have done, being what she is?*
> *Was there another Troy for her to burn?*

Later in the autumn, Maud accepted an invitation from Lilla White, daughter of the British ambassador to Turkey, to spend a month with her at the embassy. Lucien went to the boat at Marseilles to bid her farewell and gave her a small monkey which she named 'Chaperone' for fun.

Maud came of age at Christmas 1887 and discovered the truth about her father's estate. She and Kathleen shared a trust he had set up in 1865 — family diamonds, real estate and a residual income. She was now financially independent, free to come and go as she pleased and to dedicate herself to the Irish cause; she also had the excitement of having a lover without the constraints or responsibilities of marriage.

Back in Paris her offer of help for the Boulangist party was taken up when Madame Juliette Adam, an extreme French Nationalist, asked her to take proposals for a treaty with Russia to St Petersburg. The papers she would carry gave an assurance of an alliance against Germany and offered French support for Russia's control of the Bosporus. Maud felt that such a treaty would help to weaken the British empire. The adventure fired her imagination and so she left immediately, with Lucien's revolver and 'Chaperone' her monkey. En route she discovered her papers were not in order and could not resist enlisting the help of the 'enemy' — a German, who smoothed her path and travelled the remainder of the journey with her. Maud delivered the papers in time but she was not well received since the Russian officer was pro-German. However, Maud had an introduction to Princess Catherine Radziwill who helped her to enjoy her visit to Russia.

Fired by her renewed interest in the Irish cause Maud returned to Ireland after this mission and visited Michael Davitt, founder of the Irish Land League, while he was serving as a Home Rule member of parliament. She told him she considered that whatever Irish rebels did to England could not be considered a crime but an act of war. (In time, this attitude coined a new word — Maudgonning — which meant fighting for a cause in a flamboyant manner. Thus she was never taken seriously as a politician.) Davitt was against burning and assassinations; he tried to channel her efforts towards countering the English propaganda that associated the Irish party with outrages.

In Dublin she stayed with the Jamesons, friends from her childhood. Ida Jameson made a pact with Maud to work for Ireland's freedom from English rule and the two women had gold rings made, each engraved with the word 'Eire' to seal their pact. At the time, it was impossible for a lady to become a member of clubs in Dublin. Through Ida, Maud met Charles Hubert Oldham, founder of the Contemporary Club. According to her biography he introduced her to the gathered gentlemen, saying: 'Maud Gonne wants to meet John O'Leary; I thought you would all like to meet Maud Gonne.' O'Leary was just back from exile and other members of the club included Douglas Hyde, AE (George Russell), J.F. Taylor and J.B. and Willie Yeats. Maud was surprised to hear that O'Leary did not approve of the Land League while Oldham did. O'Leary told her to call to the Club any time she was in Dublin and invited her to meet his sister, Ellen. Later, he and Oldham hung pictures of Maud all around the club walls. It was a victory for Maud to be invited to a male club but O'Leary could see that her good looks and enthusiasm could be used to convert the Anglo-Irish upper-classes to the cause.

Many members of the Contemporary Club became founders of the Celtic Revival, which established a uniquely Irish cultural movement. Maud was not an intellectual, but O'Leary encouraged her to read books on Celtic mythology and Irish poetry. When Maud discovered that Ellen O'Leary had written poems, she and Oldham subsidised their publication. It was because of this new found interest in Irish poetry that Maud, with her letter of introduction, called on J.B. Yeats and his young son, the aspiring poet, Willie, that day in 1889.

# 8

*But I, being poor, have only my dreams...*
*Tread softly because you tread on my dreams.*

HE WISHES FOR THE CLOTHS OF HEAVEN

At their first meeting Willie fell headlong in love with Maud but she, already in love with Lucien, did not think of Willie in this light. Although Willie was a year older than Maud she referred to him as a 'boy'. How could this callow youth compare with her mature lover? The fact that he was obviously lost in admiration for her made little impression. Maud was accustomed to the adulation of many  dashing men.

How little Willie impressed her was evident when, within three months of meeting him, Maud conceived a child by Lucien. Their son, Georges, was born in January 1890. Although they had been together for some time it was suggested by Anna MacBride White that their love was not consummated until April 1889, when his political movement collapsed, and Boulanger fled to Brussels. She may have been comforting him as, in later years, she told Willie that 'sexual love was only justified by children'.

Although Maud and Lucien loved their child  he was cared for by a nurse in Paris and never intruded on Maud's public life.

Maud's beauty attracted many men and, according to Dominic Daly, on 16 December 1888, a month before she met Willie, Douglas Hyde wrote in his diary: 'To Sigersons in the evening where I saw the most dazzling woman I have ever seen: Miss Gonne, who drew every male in the room around her . . . We stayed talking until 1.30 am. My head was spinning with her beauty.'

Maud asked Hyde to teach her Irish and, despite his romance with a young singer called Frances Crofton, he met Maud regularly during February and March. He recorded such occasions in his diary — 'I stayed for lunch with her and we toasted cheese together by the fire. We talked about all sorts of things . . . We did not do much Irish' or again 'We lunched on omelettes that we made together by the fire. She was very cordial and made me a present of her portrait.' She went with him to the Theosophical Society and the Pan Celtic Society. These meetings were to peter out within two months, possibly again it was because of her pregnancy. She wrote in her autobiography: 'So Douglas Hyde never succeeded in making me an Irish speaker, any more than I succeeded in making him a revolutionist.'

This relationship could have made Willie jealous. He wrote in March to Katherine Tynan: 'Who told you that I am "taken up with Miss Gonne"? I think she is very good looking and that is all I think about her. What you say of her fondness for sensation is probably true . . . reminding me of Laura Armstrong without Laura's dash of half-insane genius . . . She interests me far more than Miss Gonne does and yet is only a myth and a symbol.'

Maud's heart was in France with Lucien and her interests were also in that country. General Boulanger had won a seat in the house of deputies in January 1889 and his followers waited, in vain, for his command to seize the government buildings. According to Levenson he said: 'Why should I seize power by illegal means when I can be sure of getting it in six months from now by the unanimous vote of all France?' The General left for a holiday with his mistress. While he was away, his League of Patriots was dissolved and, in August 1889, he was found guilty of conspiring to overthrow the government. By October 1889 only forty of his supporters were elected and this number fell to two by the following April.

Before the birth of her son in January of 1890 Maud was back in Ireland making speeches on behalf of the evicted people of the west of Ireland. On these occasions she met Willie and their friendship grew. He wrote her poems, which flattered her. He was hopelessly in love with her — he admitted as much in his *Memoirs*, but he had not told her of this love, partly through shyness and partly because he could not see her as the wife of a poor student. This was expressed in his poem *He wishes for the Cloths of Heaven*:

> Had I the heavens' embroidered cloths,
> Enwrought with golden and silver light,
> The blue and the dim and the dark cloths
> Of night and light and the half-light,
> I would spread the cloths under your feet:
> But I, being poor, have only my dreams;
> I have spread my dreams under your feet;
> Tread softly because you tread on my dreams.

Still Maud did not tell Willie about Lucien. In December 1889, Captain William O'Shea sued his wife, Kitty, for divorce and the scandal of her love affair with Parnell became public knowledge. Maud visited London that month for her sister's wedding to Captain Thomas David Pilcher. She decided to keep her own affair secret in case she suffered Parnell's fate and jeopardised her reputation as an Irish heroine.

She was too busy to notice Willie's dreams. She spent her time travelling between France, where she had Lucien and her child, England and Ireland. Willie met her at every opportunity. He marvelled at the number of dogs and birds she carried with her — even a full-grown hawk. The cages filled the carriage and because of her menagerie few other passengers joined her.

Up to this time, Maud had spoken only to small groups of political activists. Now she was asked to make her first public address, at Barrow-in-Furness, in Lancashire on behalf of Tim Harrington of the Irish Parliamentary Party. She spoke passionately of the evictions of Irish peasants from their homes for not paying their rents. She was so carried away that she burst into tears and was surprised when the audience applauded her wildly. Because of this she used the ploy again and again.

On behalf of some Donegal women whose husbands had been jailed for Land League activities, she went to meet members of the British parliament. One of these, whom she called 'Sir John' in her autobiography, fell under her spell and wanted to talk more of love than prisons. In 1890 she was in Donegal working for the evicted when 'Sir John' arrived from London to persuade her that she would do more for the Irish cause married to him, meeting people of influence and telling them about the plight of the Irish peasant. As a token of his love he gave her a diamond pendant and, without a thought for his feelings, Maud gave it to a woman facing eviction. News of this reached 'Sir John', who bought back the pendant and left, vowing not to return.

Her power over such men annoyed Willie greatly and his frustration comes out in the lines from *The Scholars*:

> *Bald heads forgetful of their sins,*
> *Old, learned, respectable bald heads*
> *Edit and annotate the lines*
> *That young men, tossing on their beds,*
> *Rhymed out in love's despair*
> *To flatter beauty's ignorant ear...*

Not all her conquests had 'bald heads'. John Morton, a young Liberal barrister offered to work for the release of Donegal prisoners as soon as he became secretary to Sir John Morley, Gladstone's cabinet secretary for Ireland. She wrote that: 'His devotion to me lasted some years and I fear it was bad for his career, but I had to encourage it for the sake of the prisoners.'

She enjoyed the power her beauty gave her over these men and used them but remained, physically, faithful to Lucien. Being his mistress rather than his wife suited her well. She felt no need to stay with him, or indeed with their child; she felt that Lucien would understand her absence as her work for the 'Cause' was so important. Understanding had its limitations, however. Lucien followed her to Ireland to see what she was doing; maybe stories of 'Sir John' or Morton had reached his ears. He got as far as Dunfanaghy, then became ill. She was furious he had followed her, but, when she heard of his illness, went to see him. His doctor said he had just escaped pneumonia. Contritely, she nursed him back to health, but by the end of the week they had quarrelled and he returned to France alone. She stayed behind to have treatment for a persistent cough.

When she was well enough Maud went back to Donegal. Willie missed her and began to hate her politics — his only rival, so he thought — as he says in *No Second Troy*:

> *Why should I blame her that she filled my days*
> *With misery, or that she would of late*
> *Have taught to ignorant men most violent ways,*
> *Or hurled the little streets upon the great,*
> *Had they but courage equal to desire? . . .*

Willie was not the only one who was annoyed by her politics — Dublin Castle thought she was responsible for undoing the evictions' campaign in Donegal and issued a warrant for her arrest. Before they had time to serve the warrant she decided to leave the country to avoid being put in jail, also she wanted to see Lucien and her baby in France. There she began to write articles about Ireland's evictions and political imprisonments. Lucien edited these and had them published in *La Revue Internationale*. Because of these articles, she was invited to speak to French Catholic societies who gave her money for her starving tenants and families of the prisoners. Through her colourful speeches and Lucien's influence she had 2,000 items printed in the French newspapers in one year. These were quoted in other countries. She was spreading the word, which certainly affected Britain's reputation abroad.

Although she continued to work for the Cause, she pined for Ireland. In December she returned and the authorities did not serve her with the dreaded warrant. She attended the formal opening of New Tipperary — just outside Tipperary town on the Limerick road — for tenants evicted from the old town. John O'Leary, who did not approve of the Land League, disclaimed her as his follower saying: 'She is no disciple of mine, she went there to show off her new bonnet.' This was untrue and unfair but was typical of the attitude of some of the Irish Nationalists who did not take her work seriously. She was never appointed to a position of authority in any of their organisations, but they exploited her beauty to make emotional, rather than intellectual, appeals for their fund-raising efforts.

# 9

*I would that we were, my beloved, white birds on the
    foam of the sea!
We tire of the flame of the meteor, before it can fade and
    flee . . .*

THE WHITE BIRDS

While Maud was busy with her political activities, Willie
joined the London Theosophists. He was very much under
the religious influence of Madame Blavatsky and soon was
included in the inner ring of students. From this he
graduated to the order of the 'Golden Dawn' and was
initiated into the circle by MacGregor Mathers.

His poetry had reached a new high level with the
publication of *The Lake Isle of Innisfree* and *The Man who
dreamed of Faeryland* in the *National Observer*, the first in
December 1890 and the second in February 1891. Later in
that year the Rhymers' Club was founded and met in an
inn in Wine Office Court off Fleet Street. The inn was
called the 'Cheshire Cheese' and poets met to talk and
evaluate one another's work.

He said that 'there is no fine literature without
nationality' and, when he met Maud on her trips through
Dublin, assured her his contribution to patriotism would
be through Irish literature.  It delighted her and she
reported this fact to Lucien, together with her own political
objectives. She told him of 'Sir John' and Morton but was
horrified when he suggested she give sexual favours for
political gain. She had always been faithful to him, despite
her trivial flirtations. Shattered by his suggestions she left
immediately for Dublin. Maud needed a friend.

She contacted Willie, and, although he had an appointment to visit his friend Charles Johnston in Down he came
to her hotel. He recorded that day in July 1891 in his

*Memoirs*: 'At first sight of her as she came through the door, her great height seeming to fill it, I was over-whelmed with emotion, an intoxication of pity. She did not seem to have any beauty, her face was wasted, the form of her bones showing, and there was no life in her manner. As our talk became intimate she hinted at some unhappiness, some disillusionment. The hard old resonance had gone, and she had become gentle and indolent. I was in love once more and no longer wished to fight it. I no longer thought what kind of wife would this woman make, but of her need for protection and for peace.'

Willie's kindness and understanding surfaced. He wanted to protect her from whatever threatened her, without having to be told the details if she wished to keep them secret. Throughout his life he would behave in this fashion, never judging if she was right or wrong, even when she hurt him deeply. He thought only of her happiness.

He left for County Down to keep his appointment with Charles. Maud wrote to him of a dream she had of a past life in which they were brother and sister. He misread the message, hurried back to her and proposed for the first time. She refused but asked him for his friendship as she needed his sympathy.

In need of mothering she thought of her old nurse, Mary Anne Meredith who lived in a cottage near the Baily Lighthouse in Howth. She had been happy there as a child and Willie, at a different time, had enjoyed a period of his life at the same harbour. Eternally without money Willie borrowed ten shillings from John O'Leary to make the trip — Maud insisted on paying her own way. Nurse Meredith asked if the two were engaged!

Willie and Maud explored the Hill of Howth and she told him that if she were to choose to be a bird it would be a seagull. He wrote in *The White Birds*:

*I would that we were, my beloved, white birds on the foam of*
   *the sea!*
*We tire of the flame of the meteor, before it can fade and flee;*
*And the flame of the blue star of twilight, hung low on the*
   *rim of the sky,*
*Has awaked in our hearts, my beloved, a sadness that may*
   *not die . . .*

They spent much time together for the remainder of July. She had eased off political work for fear of arrest and he was writing a play *The Countess Cathleen* and read passages to her. It was, he said in his *Memoirs*: 'a symbol of all souls who lose their peace, or their fineness, or any beauty of the spirit in political service, but chiefly of her soul that had seemed so incapable of rest.'

During their time together Maud mentioned neither Lucien nor her child to Willie. She was trying to protect her reputation but, also, she enjoyed Willie's attention, which might not have been so wholehearted if he knew she loved another. Suddenly she had a message from Lucien. Their child was seriously ill with meningitis. She returned to France immediately, telling Willie that the Boulangists needed her and that she could not refuse their request.

Back in Paris she was distraught to find Georges near to death. She had spent little time with the child, leaving him to his nurse, and was consumed by guilt when the baby died. She and Lucian had the little body embalmed and entombed in a specially built memorial chapel. Maud went into deep morning and could not sleep. She took to using chloroform, which became a habit. She wrote to Willie that a little child she had adopted had died.

Death followed death in her life — Boulanger's mistress died in July 1891 and he committed suicide on her grave on 30 September. Another of her heroes, Parnell, died of a heart attack in Brighton. On 11 October 1891, by chance,

Maud returned to Ireland on the boat that carried his body. As usual Willie met her at the boat. He did not like crowds and would not follow the funeral but wrote a poem about the event, *Parnell's Funeral*:

> *A bundle of tempestuous cloud is blown*
> *About the sky; where that is clear of cloud*
> *Brightness remains; a brighter star shoots down . . .*

Maud, still in black for her child's death, was among the enormous crowd in Glasnevin cemetery, who saw a star fall as dusk approached. In her autobiography she wrote: 'As the thud of the earth sounded on the coffin, a rift in the leaden sky parted the clouds and a bright falling star was seen. Life out of death, life out of death eternally.'

This feeling of 'life out of death' persisted. Maud knew that Willie's beliefs accepted reincarnation so she asked Willie and AE if a child could be reincarnated of the same parents after death. Her interest in reincarnation led her to London, with Willie, where she was initiated in the Order of the Golden Dawn on 16 November 1891 in the Masons' Hall, Euston Street.

Earlier in the year she had met a Father Dissard through the Boulangists and he had asked her if she would consider becoming a Catholic. She told him that she could not because of her belief in reincarnation.

Willie was delighted with their shared membership of the Golden Dawn. 'She had come (to) have need of me . . . and I had no doubt that need would become love.' In *Words* he wrote:

> *That every year I have cried, 'At length*
> *My darling understands it all,*
> *Because I have come into my strength,*
> *And words obey my call';*

*That had she done so who can say*
*What would have shaken from the sieve?*
*I might have thrown poor words away*
*And been content to live.*

Through the spirit world Maud and her friends thought they could project themselves out of their bodies and visit one another on the 'astral level'. Once she described a visit to her sister Kathleen and nephew Toby. The rooms appeared different to their home in Ely Place in Dublin and she discovered that they had gone to Howth, as Toby was recovering from an illness.

Later she and Willie visited one another in this fashion. John O'Leary did not approve of such practices and Willie wrote to him in August 1892: 'Now as to magic, it is surely absurd to hold me "weak" or otherwise because I choose to persist in a study which I decided deliberately four or five years ago to make next to my poetry, the most important pursuit of my life . . . If I had not made magic my constant study I could not have written a single word of my Blake book, nor would *The Countess Cathleen* ever have come to exist. The mystical life is the centre of all that I do and all that I think and all that I write.' *The Countess Cathleen and Various Legends and Lyrics* were dedicated to Maud, and Yeats introduced her to the Rhymers Club.

Now that Maud had lost her own child her thoughts turned to her little half-sister Eileen Wilson. She thought that Mary Anne Meredith would make an excellent nurse for her in Howth. In 1892 a member of the Russian aristocracy was looking for a nanny to teach his children English and asked his friend Charles Dilke for help. Through Charles he met Maud Gonne who said that her companion might be suitable. Margaret Wilson, then aged about thirty-five, became nanny to Baroness Budberg. The two were devoted to one another and Margaret reared not alone Baroness Budberg but also her children. The Baroness called her Ducki and her children called her Micki. All the Budbergs spoke English and Irish first as Margaret never mastered Russian.

Although she was kind, thoughtful and pretty Margaret had no known love affairs in the forty-seven years she was with the family. They thought her spinsterish! She had no fixed wage but got what money she asked for. They thought she sent it home to Ireland.

She kept in touch with her daughter. Although she returned home to see Eileen only once during the remainder of her life she sent her a large dowry and many presents.

# 10

*But dear, cling close to me; since you were gone,*
*My barren thoughts have chilled me to the bone.*

Willie was persistent in his wooing of Maud and thought
that, eventually, she would respond. Ignorant of her association with Lucien, he assumed she was so taken up with
the cause of Ireland that she subdued any sexual inclina-
tions and she encouraged him to believe this as she
depended on his friendship and devotion.

Her form of Nationalism was different to his. She
visited both the people who were being evicted and the
political prisoners and gathered first-hand accounts of per-
secutions to be used at her constant public appearances.
She had no reservations about the use of force. Her father
had fought and killed for his beliefs and she considered
the Irish struggle a just war.

Willie, on the other hand, rarely met the common people. She called him a snob. He wrote about Ireland but
only the wealthy had the money or the time to read poetry.
Certainly he was accepted in literary circles but he had
little money and could not afford to follow Maud to and
from France. This kept the secret of her lover from him
and from the Irish people as a whole.

Lucien had followed her to Ireland only once and she
fed him a similar story to the one she told Willie — the
Cause was all important and time consuming, which
would account for her long absences.

In January 1892 Maud was once more in Paris to
raise money. In an article Willie wrote: 'She takes her
audience . . . from the bloodless conversion of pagan
Ireland . . . down to our own day, and the death of
Parnell, and every event is described as vividly and

48

simply as if it were all in some famous ballad of old unhappy far-off things, and battles long ago.'

L'Association du St Patrice, founded by John O'Leary, held a banquet in Paris on 17 March 1892 and Maud was the only woman to be invited. Again she spoke of the evictions and of the conditions of Irish prisoners.

Willie hated her political career because it caused them to be separated. In May 1892 he, and T.W. Rolleston, the poet, formed the National Literary Society in Dublin. It had affiliations with Young Ireland groups throughout the country. Lending libraries were formed which made Irish publications available to all classes of people and helped to spread a truly Irish culture. Willie was delighted when Maud gave up her rooms in Paris to help with this work and she proposed setting up a cottage industry to sell Irish tweed in France. The Literary Society seemed to unite all shades of Nationalists and it was a very happy time for both Maud and Willie. Their names were linked all over the country. He proposed to her again and was declined once more.

Willie's longing for a new and better literature was not fully supported by Maud and the barrister J.F. Taylor, who saw nothing wrong with the old hackneyed verses. Maud and Willie quarrelled and before their differences could be resolved she became ill once more with a lung congestion. She was attended by the Nationalist, Dr George Sigerson, who banned all visitors. One of her followers came to Nassau Street to nurse her and allegedly spread a nasty rumour that she had been Willie's lover and had had an abortion. When Willie heard it he was very upset and went to Sligo to seek refuge. She was too ill to deny the charges and her cousin May came from London to make arrangements to take her back to Paris. Willie could not work without her and was very concerned that she left under such dreadful circumstances. In *Reconciliation* he said:

*Some may have blamed you that you took away*
*The verses that could move them on the day*
*When, the ears being deafened, the sight of the eyes*
*    blind*
*With lightning, you went from me, and I could find*
*Nothing to make a song about but kings,*
*Helmets, and swords, and half-forgotten things*
*That were like memories of you — but now*
*We'll out, for the world lives as long ago;*
*And while we're in our laughing, weeping fit,*
*Hurl helmets, crowns and swords into the pit.*
*But, dear, cling close to me; since you were gone,*
*My barren thoughts have chilled me to the bone.*

Willie followed her to Paris in February 1894 and stayed with MacGregor Mathers, who had initiated him into the Golden Dawn. Maud was not in the best of health when she showed him around her beloved Paris. They went to see *Axel*, a play by Villiers de l'Isle-Adam, which she translated for him. Willie returned to London with a happy heart. A month later, on 29 March, his play *The Land of Heart's Desire*, written for Maud, opened as a curtain raiser for John Todhunter's *Comedy of Sighs* at the Avenue Theatre and outlived the latter.

While she was showing Willie around Paris Maud was, again, pregnant by Lucien. He had been shattered by the death of both his child and his idol Boulanger, and also, by the loss of his own political position. She persuaded him to apply for the editorship of *La Patrie*, a newspaper run by the owner of *Les Printemps* department stores. This restored his self confidence. They had a romantic reunion in the Auvergne and she explained her belief that their child could be reincarnated. Always dramatic, she suggested this union should take place in the vault below the memorial chapel built for Georges. With her theosophic beliefs she would have planned some form of ritual. The macabre scene may have been helped with a little hashish, which she was known to have used at the time. Maybe, indeed, the cold, damp, morbid surroundings were forgotten in sudden passion — she cherished the belief that her daughter, Iseult, who was born on 6 August 1894, was conceived in that sacred place.

Nancy Cardozo, in her biography of Maud says that she had a romantic reunion with Lucien and was living with him at the time. She told Willie that the conception was the result of a once-off occasion, endured rather than enjoyed, to replace her dead child. When, as an old woman, she wrote her autobiography, she would say that she was in love with, rather than the lover of, Lucien. Iseult, she would say, was adopted.

Although she had been consumed with guilt because she had spent little time with Georges, shortly after baby Iseult was born she announced that she must go back to her work for Ireland. Her restless spirit drove her on. She visualised herself in the role of politician, a predominantly male role in her time. If a male politician left his new-born child with servants to engage in political work for a cause he would not be faulted. She did not count the cost of leaving Iseult and Lucien.

# 11

*Beloved, let your eyes half close, and your heart beat*
*Over my heart, and your hair fall over my breast,*
*Drowning love's lonely hour in deep twilight of rest . . .*

While Maud was pregnant with Iseult she did not travel as much as usual. She had refused Willie's proposals of marriage and he yearned for her. At almost thirty years of age he records in his *Memoirs* that his friends 'had all mistresses of one kind or another and that most, at need, went home with harlots . . . I had never since childhood kissed a woman's lips. At Hammersmith I saw a woman of the town walking up and down in the empty railway station. I thought of offering myself to her, but the old thought came back, "No, I love the most beautiful woman in the world".' At a 'Yellow Book' dinner in April 1894 he noticed Olivia Shakespear. She was a cousin of Lionel Johnson, one of his literary friends, and he arranged a meeting between the two in June of that year. She had liked Willie's play *The Land of Heart's Desire* and he told her of his love for Maud Gonne. She was unhappily married to a solicitor, Henry Hope Shakespear, and the two compared their unhappy love lives. They exchanged letters when he went to Sligo during the winter of 1894-95.

Willie decided that if he could not get the woman he loved it would be a comfort, even for a little while, to devote himself to another. The first step was to leave home at Bedford Road and move in to Fountain Court with Arthur Symons, a member of the Rhymers Club. One evening when Symons was out Willie invited Olivia back to the house. He went out to buy cakes for the tea and forget his key. A man had to climb through the attic window to let him in and this brought an end to the planned seduction. When Symons returned, Willie spent the rest of the night talking about Maud Gonne.

Maud heard of this attempted seduction and sent word to Willie that she had seen an apparition of him, standing in her room that evening — a call to heel of her straying admirer!

In April 1895, Willie was on holiday with Douglas Hyde and discovered Castle Rock Island in Lough Key, County Roscommon. He enquired about the cost of hiring it and, when he found the rent was not high, he took it with the hope of making it an Irish Eleusis for Maud and himself.

Maud found the idea exciting and seemed to have no difficulty in leaving Lucien and Iseult. She would have given politics as the reason for her absence. Willie said that although they met for political reasons politics were soon forgotten and they enjoyed a sense of intimacy.

According to Maud and Willie their castle in Lough Key was filled with invisible spirits with whom they could communicate and who would tell them the meaning of the universe and the scriptures. They called it the 'Castle of Heroes' and invited close friends to make suggestions for the founding of a mystical order. They communicated with ancient Irish people or gods to give them strength to free Ireland. Their friend MacGregor Mathers and his wife helped them with rituals and Willie hoped to invite Irish men and women to join in their worship.

He and Maud took hashish to heighten their fantasies and kept a record of these in a notebook. Yet, despite all their intimacies, Willie's hope of a sexual relationship seemed as remote as ever.

He had kept in contact with Olivia and in March 1896 they decided to rent a flat in Woburn Buildings to live together. She went with him to Tottenham Court Road to buy a bed and discovered that each inch added to the cost, which was an important factor for Willie as he had little money.

Nervous at first, Willie could not consummate the affair, and they merely talked over tea. On the third evening his nervousness disappeared and they enjoyed a good sexual relationship over a period of a year. In his writings he referred to her as 'Diana Vernon' and wrote her many beautiful love poems including *He Bids His Beloved Be at Peace*:

> *Beloved, let your eyes half close, and your heart beat*
> *Over my heart, and your hair fall over my breast,*
> *Drowning love's lonely hour in deep twilight of rest,*
> *And hiding their tossing manes and their tumultuous feet.*

He admired her 'perfect Greek features,' her love of simple pleasures' and the fact that she was a good listener. To produce a romantic atmosphere, he would read love poems before she visited him. One day she found him with a letter rather than a love poem in his hand and asked him if there was someone else in his life.

Maud heard of the liaison. She wrote to Willie to say that she was in London and would like to meet him for a meal. This heralded the end to the affair with Olivia.

In *The Lover Mourns for the Loss of Love* he says:

> *I had a beautiful friend*
> *And dreamed that the old despair*
> *Would end in love in the end:*
> *She looked in my heart one day*
> *And saw your image was there;*
> *She has gone weeping away.*

He felt that she was too near his soul, too salutary and wholesome to his inmost being. Olivia left him, but within a short time they exchanged letters.

They remained very close friends and their correspondence continued until Olivia's death in 1938.

# 12

*O do not love too long,*
*Or you will grow out of fashion . . .*

O DO NOT LOVE TOO LONG

After he met Olivia Willie spent the winter in Sligo. It was the first time he was accepted there as a poet rather than as a relative of the Pollexfens. He was invited to spend a few days in Lissadell, the home of the Gore-Booth family and there met the two daughters, Eva and Constance:

*The light of evening, Lissadell,*
*Great windows, open to the south,*
*Two girls in silk kimonos, both*
*Beautiful, one a gazelle . . .*

While Constance reminded him of Maud Gonne, Eva became his friend.

His newfound habit of socialising continued when he visited Sligo again in the summer of 1896 with Arthur Symons, and, having seen the sights including Ben Bulben they went to Galway to stay in Tulira Castle with Edward Martyn. Lady Isabella Augusta Gregory, Martyn's near neighbour, called to Tulira in August and Willie made her acquaintance

Lady Gregory was the twelfth child of a family of sixteen, born to a Protestant landowner called Persse. When she was 28 she married Sir William Gregory, a former governor of Ceylon. He was nearly forty years her senior and although it was not a love match they had a very good relationship.

Shortly after the birth of her son, Robert, Augusta met, and fell in love with, Wilfred Blunt. They had an eight month love affair and she wrote him twelve love sonnets.

The affair came to an end when her husband and his wife became aware of the situation. She continued to love him although he had many other women in his life. When he died in 1922 he left her his bible, which, in time, was buried with her.

When she met Willie she was a forty-five year old widow and her son Robert was at Harrow. She was busy editing her husband's autobiography and had begun to collect Irish folklore. She lived at Coole Park, which took its name from the lake at the edge of the woods surrounding it. She invited Willie and Symons to lunch on two occasions and Willie stayed on for a few days when Symons returned to London. She wanted to play a part in the Irish movement and Willie encouraged her to continue with her interest in folk tales. She took up playwriting and had a flair for comedies which were well received. Coole became noted for its literary meetings and a large copper beech testifies to this day to the many famous guests who carved their names on its trunk — W.B.Y., G.B.S, AE, J.M.S. (Synge) A.J. (Augustus John). Willie was a frequent guest and found great peace there. He was always welcome but was never overfamiliar with his hostess. In the many letters exchanged between the two she addressed him as 'My dear Willie' while he always used the more formal 'My dear Lady Gregory'. He visited her in her London flat in the winter of 1896 and told her of his great love for Maud Gonne. With a love affair in her own past she sympathised with him.

In December, he went to Paris to work with Maud on the ritual for the 'Castle of Heroes'. He stayed at the Hotel Corneille and heard that upstairs lived a student, John Millington Synge, who had studied languages, including Irish, at Trinity College, Dublin. Willie and Maud introduced themselves to him.

On New Year's Day 1897, Maud and Willie launched a Paris branch of the Young Ireland Society, 'L'Association

Irlandaise'. On one of Synge's visits to Maud on the Avenue d'Eylau, he was persuaded to join this association but, as he was opposed to the use of physical force in the struggle for freedom, he soon withdrew as an active member. Willie suggested that Synge concentrate on Irish literature and advised him to go to the Aran islands to record the culture of the island people, a venture never before undertaken. By the end of January the hotel proved too expensive for Willie and he had to return to London and to Olivia, with whom he was living at the time.

Maud started a monthly publication called *L'Irlande Libre*, with her usual theme of Irish politics and deprivation of the tenants. She decided to go to America to raise funds for the centenary of the 1798 Irish Rising but was not given authorisation by the Dublin Committee. Maud followed Willie to London to look for help.

Soon Maud was back dominating his thoughts: 'I saw much of Maud Gonne and my hope renewed again. If I could go to her and prove, by putting my hand in the fire till I had burnt it badly, would not that make her understand that devotion like mine should {not} be thrown away.' With her persuasion, he allowed his name to go forward as President of the Centenary Association for Great Britain and France. He thought, when elected, that he could steer it away from Fenianism.

Queen Victoria was to celebrate her diamond jubilee, and, when in March 1897, John O'Leary chaired a meeting in Dublin to make plans for the Irish 1798 centenary, James Connolly of the Irish Socialist Party, took charge of protesting against any Irish celebrations for the queen. Willie persuaded Maud to speak at Connolly's meeting in College Green on 20 June, the evening before the jubilee. On the day itself, Pat O'Brien showed slides of Irish prisoners and eviction scenes from the window of the Nationalist Club in Parnell Square. Carrying a black coffin, marked

'British Empire' Connolly and his followers marched through the streets. Just before they were arrested the coffin was thrown into the river Liffey. Next morning Maud arrived at the Bridewell to pay Connolly's fine and to raise bail for the others. She contacted Tim Harrington and asked him to defend them.

For the 1798 centenary committee, she and Willie, both members of the IRB, toured the midlands of England and Scotland. From this tour he wrote to Lady Gregory: 'After the meeting this morning Miss Gonne and myself went to the picture gallery to see a Rossetti that is there. She is very kind and friendly, but whether more than that I cannot tell':

> Sweetheart, do not love too long:
> I loved long and long,
> And grew to be out of fashion
> Like an old song.
>
> All through the years of our youth
> Neither could have known
> Their own thought from the other's
> We were so much at one.
>
> But O, in a minute she changed —
> O do not love too long,
> Or you will grow out of fashion
> Like an old song.

Maud told Willie that she was tired and needed a rest. She went back to France, where Lucien and Iseult were waiting for her. With her cousin May she visited Aix les Bains casino where she won enough to pay for the defence of Connolly's followers.

Her restless spirit drove her on and in the autumn of 1897 she left for America on the Cunard Liner, the *Lucania*.

On her tour her beauty and striking speeches aroused sympathy for the Wolfe Tone 1798 Commemoration and she returned with £1,000 for the fund. Never resting for long she travelled all over Ireland from Ballina to Tralee to Dublin making speech after speech at endless meetings.

# 13

*I have drunk ale from the Country of the Young
And weep because I know all things now . . .*
HE THINKS OF HIS PAST GREATNESS WHEN A PART OF THE
CONSTELLATIONS OF HEAVEN

In his *Memoirs* Willie describes his spiritual marriage to Maud. On one of the Maud's visits to Dublin in 1898 she stayed at her usual hotel on Nassau Street. When Willie called to see her she asked him if he had had a strange dream and he said that he had dreamed that, for the first time, she had kissed him. She explained that she too dreamed: 'When I fell asleep last night I saw, standing at my bedside, a great spirit. He took me to a great throng of spirits, and you were among them. My hand was put in yours and I was told we were married. After that I remembered nothing.' Then she kissed him 'with the bodily mouth' to seal their 'spiritual marriage'. (In her biography of Maud, Nancy Cardozo explained that spiritual unions were not unusual at that time. G.B. Shaw and May Morris shared one.)

The following morning Maud told him that she should not have behaved in that fashion as she could never be his real wife. At last she began to tell him of Lucien. Her version emphasised that she and Lucien shared nationalistic ideals for both Ireland and France. She did not stress the love affair but told him, none-the-less, that they had the child who died. He knew of her sorrow at the death of that child and she reminded him of their talk of reincarnating a child from the same parents. 'She had gone to him in the vault under the memorial chapel. A girl child was born, now two years old. Since the child's birth I understand her to say amid so much broken speech, she and Millevoye had lived apart' because she added, she had a horror of sex. Willie accepted this explanation, although he knew she did not tell him the full story because it was too painful for her.

In *He thinks of his Past Greatness When a Part of the Constellations of Heaven* he wrote:

> *I have drunk ale from the Country of the Young*
> *And weep because I know all things now:*
> *I have been a hazel-tree, and they hung*
> *The Pilot Star and the Crooked Plough*
> *Among my leaves in times out of mind:*
> *I became a rush that horses tread:*
> *I became a man, a hater of the wind,*
> *Knowing one, out of all things, alone that his head*
> *May not lie on the breast nor lips on the hair*
> *Of the woman that he loves, until he dies.*
> *O beast of the wilderness, bird of the air,*
> *Must I endure your amorous cries?*

In his *Memoirs* he continued: '. . . in all that followed I was careful to touch as one might a sister. If she was to come to me it must be from no temporary passionate impulse but the approval of her conscience.'

She said she stayed with Lucien because 'she did not know what would happen to him if her influence was not there.' This, again, was a half truth. Lucien needed her help when Boulanger died but by this time Lucien was a successful editor.

She left for Paris and Willie followed her. He wrote to Lady Gregory: 'I don't know whether things are well or ill with me, in some ways ill, for she had been almost cold with me though she has made it easy for me to see her. If you knew all . . . you would understand why this love has been so bitter a thing to me, and why things I have known lately have made it, in a certain sense, the bitterer and the harder.'

Lady Gregory was not taken in so easily. She felt that Maud was very selfish and was only playing with Willie. She wrote to a friend saying, with tongue in cheek, that she did not wish Maud ill but quoted an old Irish saying: 'God is unjust if she dies a quiet death'.

Willie went back to Coole once again, for mental and physical comfort. Lady Gregory said she thought and treated him as if he were her son, but even her kindness was not enough. He said that he was: 'tortured by physical desire and disappointed love. Often as I walked in the woods at Coole, it would have been a relief to have screamed aloud.'

When Maud came back to Nassau Street, Lady Gregory was determined to have it out with her. She bluntly asked Maud what her intentions were towards Willie and Maud, who thought it was no concern of Lady Gregory's, said that neither she nor Willie were the 'marrying sort' as they had more things on their minds.

Willie was appreciative of all that Lady Gregory did to help yet he could not stop loving Maud. In a poem called *Friends* he spoke of his relationships with Maud, Lady Gregory and Olivia Shakespear:

> *Now must I these three praise —*
> *Three women that have wrought*
> *What joy is in my days:*
> *One because no thought,*
> *Nor those unpassing cares,*
> *No, not in these fifteen*
> *Many-times-troubled years,*
> *Could ever come between*
> *Mind and delighted mind;*
> *And one because her hand*
> *Had strength that could unbind*
> *What none can understand,*

*What none can have and thrive,*
*Youth's dreamy load, till she*
*So changed me that I live*
*Labouring in ecstasy.*
*And what of her that took*
*All till my youth was gone*
*With scarce a pitying look?*
*How could I praise that one?*
*When day begins to break*
*I count my good and bad,*
*Being wakeful for her sake,*
*Remembering what she had,*
*What eagle look still shows,*
*While up from my heart's root*
*So great a sweetness flows*
*I shake from head to foot.*

# 14

*I thought my dear must her own soul destroy,*
*So did fanaticism and hate enslave it . . .*

THE CIRCUS ANIMALS' DESERTION

When Maud said she had more on her mind than marrying, at that time, she was speaking the truth. She was
interested in a periodical, revived in 1899 by Arthur
Griffith, called *The United Irishman*. In its first issue on 4
March it declared that British law had no place in Ireland.
*The United Irishman's* objective was to have an all-Irish
State, governed by Irish people. This was the Nationalism
that appealed to Maud. She undertook to pay Griffith 25
shillings a week, which was the only salary he took as
editor and with which he paid his mother for his keep. In
return Griffith reported on Maud's various political
activities and speeches.

*The United Irishman* gave details of a candidate to rep-
resent South Mayo in parliament – John MacBride 'a ruddy
faced, red-haired man'. 'Still on the battlefield of South
Africa fighting the Boer War', MacBride was born in
Westport, County Mayo in 1869. His brother, Anthony, a
London doctor, was active in several Nationalist groups.
In time, John became a chemist's assistant in Dublin and
joined the Celtic Literary Society. Around 1896 he had
gone to South Africa as an assayer and was credited with
being foremost in the founding of the Irish Brigade formed
to fight the British. Arthur Griffith, also in South Africa,
was a member and although John MacBride did not boast
of his own bravery, Arthur Griffith and fellow officers
spoke very highly of his courage in action. Indeed Griffith
wrote a verse in which he described him as 'fearless John
MacBride.' Maud read this article and sent John MacBride
two telegrams of support. Willie, too, was enthusiastic, and

suggested that his rival in the elections, Tim Harrington, should withdraw.

Meanwhile, Willie had rewritten *The Countess Cathleen* and it was produced on 8 May, 1899 in Dublin's Ancient Concert Rooms. He tried to persuade Maud to take the leading role but she was too busy. However, she became one of the guarantors for the production. The play received much acclaim as a cultural event, but the Catholic Church condemned it because it told of a countess who sold her soul to demons to save her people from famine.

In *The Circus Animals' Desertion* Yeats wrote:

> And then a counter-truth filled out its play,
> The Countess Cathleen *was the name I gave it;*
> *She, pity-crazed, had given her soul away,*
> *But masterful heaven had intervened to save it . . .*

The performance was to sow the seeds for the Abbey Theatre, but it also was a turning point in the relationship between Maud and Willie. He was to devote himself to cultural nationalism while she would follow a political path.

In the spring of 1900 Queen Victoria came to Dublin. Addresses of welcome were the order of the day and a 'Treat' was organised for children in the Phoenix Park. This annoyed Maud so she and a priest, Father Anderson, organised a counter attraction provided by the ladies Committee of the Patriotic Children's Treat. Maud advertised in newspapers and got support from all sides. Ginger beer, cakes, sweets, sandwiches were freely donated and about 30,000 children took part. They headed for Clontarf Park in lorries, under the direction of young men from the Gaelic Athletic Association and the Celtic Literary Society. A friend, Mary Quinn, helped Maud to control the children who carried green branches.

Willie's fears were expressed in his description of the same event in his autobiography: 'In a field beyond Drumcondra, and in the presence of a priest of their church, they swear to cherish towards England, until the freedom of Ireland has been won, undying enmity. How many of these children will carry bomb or rifle when a little under or a little over thirty?' In *The Circus Animals' Desertion* he said:

> *I thought my dear must her own soul destroy*
> *So did fanaticism and hate enslave it,*
> *And this brought forth a dream and soon enough*
> *This dream itself had all my thought and love . . .*

Maud was delighted with this venture and founded the 'Daughters of Erin' whose aim was to give classes in Irish history, Irish music, Irish dancing and the Irish language to Irish children. Mary Quinn became the secretary of the Daughters of Erin. Arthur Griffith, Pádraig Colum, AE and indeed Willie were persuaded to give talks to the group and Pádraig Pearse examined the children in Irish. Although Willie condemned any incitement to violence he could see the value of educational work.

In July of that same year Maud left Dublin for France with a delegation from the Transvaal Committee. Lucien welcomed them in an editorial in *La Patrie*. Celebrations for Bastille Day were taking place and the secretary of the Opera invited the visiting committee to a performance of *The Valkyrie*. They could not stay for this but Maud, Lucien and Madame de Ste Croix took up the invitation. During the performance, Lucien said he knew of a young lady who had a better voice than the female lead. This drew a remark from Madame de Ste Croix that Maud had been away from Paris too long.

Some days later Maud left for a holiday with her sister in Switzerland. Lucien asked if he could join her and she agreed. She had read an article in *La Patrie* saying that Germany was the enemy of France, while no mention was made of England. Puzzled she asked Lucien who had written the article and he said it was a woman who had as great love for Alsace-Lorraine as Maud had for Ireland.

In *A Servant of the Queen* she wrote: 'For a long while I did not speak. I gazed at those cruel snow mountains, which were turning my heart into stone in spite of the scent of flowers and the hum of wild bees around us, whispering of life . . . "You need not tell me the name of the writer of that article. It is the singer you wanted to bring me to see in Paris, a friend of Clemenceau. He has triumphed at last, through her, and broken our alliance. Goodbye old friend, I go my way alone and carry on the fight".'

Lucien had been unfaithful to both parts of their alliance, the physical and the political. Lucien, who had been the love of her life for thirteen years, and to whom she had been faithful, Lucien who was the father of her two children had left her for another woman. What Madame de Ste Croix had said was true. Maud had been away too often and too long from Paris. She had not expected this and was completely lost. If she had not a good sexual relationship with him she would not have been so upset. If, as she told Willie, she had an aversion to sex, she would not have minded that Lucien took another lover as she could have still used him to help politically. To compound matters when a French officer on intelligence work in London, with a letter of introduction from Maud to the IRB, was betrayed Lucien blamed Maud. The officer was arrested and returned to Paris. Maud asked Willie to help unravel the problem, caused by an internal weakness in the IRB and both resigned from the organisation. Despite this Lucien said he and his party could never trust the Irish again and that she had finished all her work for France. This was the final blow. Their only link now was through their daughter Iseult.

Iseult had been in the care of the Carmelite nuns in Laval. Their chaplain, Maud's old friend, had been elevated to Canon Dissard. Nurse Mary Anne Meredith retired and Eileen, Maud's half-sister, who had grown up with the Gonne good looks, was sent to Paris to learn French. Both girls were left in the charge of an elderly widow, Madame de Bourbonne. Although there was a gap of ten years between their ages Iseult and Eileen must have felt a kinship. Both were reared by nannies or nurses. While Maud had money and could afford to keep Iseult, Eileen's mother, Margaret Wilson, had to give up her daughter and take the offer of work as a governess to Baron Budberg's family in Russia. She kept in contact with her daughter by letter and Baroness Moura Budberg's father visited Eileen in Paris and brought her messages from her mother.

# 15

*Did that play of mine send out*
*Certain men the English shot?*
*Did words of mine put too great strain*
*On that woman's reeling brain? . . .*

MAN AND THE ECHO

Within a few months of breaking up with Lucien Maud was on the platform of the Gare de Lyon in Paris to meet John MacBride on his return from the Boer War. Arthur Griffith introduced him to her and to other members of the Paris branch of the Young Ireland Society.

When the others left, Maud, John and Griffith dined together and stayed up all night talking. John had been involved in guerrilla warfare, which, he felt, might help Ireland. He could not return to Ireland as he might be arrested by the British. Maud, John and Griffith debated how best John could serve the cause and decided that he should visit America. He was a soldier rather than an orator so Maud and Griffith visited him again the following day to help formulate his speeches.

He left for America, but, as he feared, he lacked experience in public-speaking. He wrote to Maud asking her to come and join him as 'Clan na Gael' were willing to promote a joint tour. She accepted willingly. Queen Victoria died on 22 January 1901, and when Maud disembarked from the French liner *La Champagne* in New York on 10 February to join John, she told journalists that Irishmen had little reason to mourn the dead queen. A voice from her past, Lucien echoed these sentiments in an article in *La Patrie*.

She toured America with John and he spoke of the Boer War while she condemned the United Irish League which advocated that Irishmen should unite to speed — Home

Rule — self government within the empire. Maud favoured more militant steps and her condemnation was not well received.

John's speeches improved with Maud's help and he was no longer dependent on notes. He wrote to his mother: 'Miss Gonne astonishes me the way in which she can stand the knocking about. For a woman it is wonderful'. Not exactly romantic words but Maud in *A Servant of the Queen* said that he proposed to her in America. Certainly he thought well of her but the proposal may have been an exaggeration as she needed an admirer to make up for the fact that Lucien had left her for another woman.

When Arthur Griffith wrote to ask her to come home because his co-editor Rooney was not well, she returned immediately. Back in London, she was weary from all the travelling. She and Willie dined with her sister Kathleen Pilcher. He complimented Kathleen on her dress and on keeping her looks. She said that it took hard work — a theme Willie used in the poem *Adam's Curse*:

> . . . *To be born woman is to know* . . .
> *That we must labour to be beautiful* . . .
> *It's certain there is no fine thing*
> *Since Adam's fall but needs much labouring* . . .

Continuing in the same poem Willie shows that he was weary of rejection:

> *We sat grown quiet at the name of love;*
> *We saw the last embers of daylight die,*
> *And in the trembling blue-green of the sky*
> *A moon, worn as if it had been a shell*
> *Washed by time's waters as they rose and fell*
> *About the stars and broke in days and years.*

*I had a thought for no one's but your ears:*
*That you were beautiful, and that I strove*
*To love you in the old high way of love;*
*That it had all seemed happy, and yet we'd grown*
*As weary-hearted as that hollow moon.*

The day following the visit to Kathleen, Willie and Maud were in Westminster Abbey. He asked why she did not not care for herself as Kathleen did, yet he told her she was more beautiful than anyone he had known. Again he asked her to marry him — to give up politics and to live a peaceful life with him among his writer and artist friends.

She enquired if he would ever tire of asking that question and said he would not be happy with her, that poets should never marry. His beautiful poetry came from his unhappiness. Marriage would be dull, she said, but she valued his friendship, which he gave when she most needed it. Her life centred around the work she did — and she lived life while others merely existed.

Why should she marry him? She had never been physically attracted to him. To give up politics was the last thing she wanted as she delighted in her public life. She had as much as she wanted of the company of writers and artists and their appreciation was shown in the many portraits painted and poems written about her. Most, including Willie, had not a penny to their names.

They were near the Stone of Destiny and she asked him if he could get it back to their Castle of Heroes in Lough Key. This distracted him and also accentuated what they had in common thus softening the blow of yet another refusal.

Willie's family were on the move again in 1901. His mother had died in 1900 on one of his visits home and now friends organised a Dublin exhibition of the paintings of J.B. and Nathaniel Hone. J.B. and family, without Willie, moved to Dublin, Lily to continue her craftwork and help set up the Dun Emer Industries. Evolving from the Dun Emer Industries Lolly helped to establish the Cuala Press which printed much of Willie's work. Sarah Purser helped with Jack's painting career.

Willie kept on his apartment in Woburn Buildings but continued to work in Ireland with Lady Gregory, George Moore, Edward Martyn and J.M. Synge to form an Irish Literary Theatre with Maud as patron.

Maud had moved to 25, Coulson Avenue, Rathgar, and her house became a meeting place for Nationalists whom Willie distrusted. AE was her neighbour and had become involved in the Irish Agriculture Organisation Society, which set up co-operatives to help farmers. Both he and Maud regretted the fact that Willie neglected his poetry because of his interest in theatre.

The Irish Literary Theatre employed the Benson Company to present a double bill at the Gaiety in Dublin on 21 October, 1901. The plays were *Diarmuid and Grania* by Willie and George Moore and *Casadh an tSúgain* (*The Twisting of the Rope*) from a story by Willie, rewritten for the stage by Douglas Hyde. Lady Gregory had helped with writing both and was present at all performances, apart from one evening when she gave a reception for an Art Exhibition by Jack Yeats. She wrote a review of the exhibition which was published in American papers. This review was noticed by John Quinn, a wealthy American lawyer, who was endeavouring to trace his Irish roots. He made contact with the group and their relationship grew stronger over the years.

October 1901 was the first time a play in Irish was performed in the Gaiety Theatre. Douglas Hyde had founded the Gaelic League and girls from the organisation sang Irish songs at the interval. Maud and Willie arrived at the opening by cab. The public were so excited that an attempt was made to unhitch the horse from the cab so that the crowd could pull them along by hand to a supper party. Maud prevented them but this euphoria removed some of her doubts about the theatre.

Willie, again with help from Lady Gregory, wrote *Cathleen ni Houlihan*, a play about the French expedition to Killala Bay to aid the Irish rebellion of 1798. In it a young man is about to be married, when an old woman persuades him that he has a fate higher than marriage. He is destined to die for Ireland and the old woman was, of course, Ireland herself. Maud agreed to play the part.

Soon she got word that her old nurse, Mary Anne Meredith had died. In appreciation of her devotion to the whole family, Maud had her buried near the family grave in Tongham where her gravestone had the inscription 'Beloved nurse of Colonel Gonne's children, 19–10–1831 — 17–2–1902.' This was a fitting way of thanking her for rearing Maud, Kathleen and Eileen.

That same month of February Maud took off from rehearsals to lecture in Paris with John MacBride but wrote to Willie saying how pleased she was with the play and with the involvement of the Fay brothers. She was back in Dublin in March but insisted on playing the part as she thought fit and would not take direction. The cast celebrated Lady Gregory's fiftieth birthday on 15 March.

*Cathleen ni Houlihan* was produced as part of a double bill with AE's *Deirdre* and opened at St Theresa's Total Abstinence Hall on 2 April 1902. Maud arrived late, walked through the packed audience and then gave a superb performance. She identified with the part, which stirred deep Nationalistic feelings. William Fay said that no one else could ever play the part so well. Willie had not counted on such an effect. The play made him into a patriotic hero. This worried him and many years later he wrote, in a poem called *Man and the Echo*:

*I lie awake night after night*
*And never get the answer right.*
*Did that play of mine send out*
*Certain men the English shot?*
*Did words of mine put too great strain*
*On that woman's reeling brain? . . .*

# 16

NEVER GIVE ALL THE HEART

Lucien had left Maud for another woman in late 1900. During the following three years Maud was very busy with her political career and, many times, came in contact with John MacBride. Since his return from America he had worked as secretary to Laffan's Bureau in Paris for a salary of £2 a week. Together he and Maud addressed meetings. Like Lucien, he was in her father's image, a man of action, a soldier known for his bravery. She was thirty-six, John was younger but he seemed a suitable marriage partner as she was physically attracted to him. She may have wanted to show Lucien that she, too, could have another love. A visit she made to John for tea in his attic room in the Rue Gay de Lussac caused gossip. Willie, however, took little notice of her frequent meetings with John. Had she not told him that she had a horror of physical love?

On 14 February 1903 an item in *The United Irishman* read: 'Forthcoming event which has occasioned great interest and pleasure amongst Irish Nationalists: Miss Gonne, who some time ago became a Catholic, will, formally be received into the Catholic Church on Tuesday, at the Chapel des Dames de St Therese, Laval, and her marriage will take place before the end of the month.' She had resigned from the Order of the Golden Dawn because she thought it was associated with the Freemasons. In her autobiography she says it was through Canon Dissard and not because of her approaching marriage that she came to the Catholic Church.

In the same autobiography she tells of the mounting opposition to her marriage. Arthur Griffith wrote: 'Queen, forgive me. John MacBride, after Willie Rooney, is the best friend I ever had; you are the only woman friend I have. I only think of both your happiness. For your own sakes and for the sake of Ireland to whom you both belong, don't get married. I know you both, you are so unconventional a law to yourself; John so full of conventions. You will not be happy for long. Forgive me, but think while there is still time.'

Joseph MacBride, John's older brother, wrote: 'I think it most unwise, Maud Gonne is older than you. She is accustomed to money and you have none; she is used to going her own way and listens to no one. These are not good qualifications for a wife. A man should not marry unless he can keep his wife . . .'

While she rested, the evening before the wedding, Maud thought she heard her dead father saying: 'Lambkin, don't do it. You must not get married.' Her daughter, little Iseult, burst into tears when she heard the news.

Despite these forebodings, Maud, dressed in 'a simple costume of electric blue' became the bride of John MacBride at the Church of St Honore d'Eylau, Paris on 21 February 1903. The former chaplain to the Irish Brigade, Father Van Hecke, arrived from Belgium to perform the ceremony and spoke of the Nationalist aspirations of the bride and groom. The bride gave the final toast — 'To the complete independence of Ireland'.

Maud wrote to Lady Gregory: 'I was married at the English consulate as well as at my parish church so I think it is quite legal. We had heard there was a possibility of the English trying to arrest Major MacBride at the consulate, but I do not think it would have been really possible, as even if the consulate is English territory, which is doubtful, they couldn't have imprisoned him there for long and once outside he would have been free. No such attempt was made.'

She could not tell Willie. Later as he was about to address a public meeting in Dublin he was handed a message from Maud telling him that she had married John MacBride in Paris. He delivered the lecture but could not remember a word of it later.

Most people quote the poem *Reconciliation* when mentioning this event:

> *When the ears being deafened, the sight of the eyes*
> *    blind,*
> *With lightning, you went from me . . .*

but there is hope at the end of that poem:

> *But dear cling close to me; since you were gone,*
> *My barren thoughts have chilled me to the bone.*

Willie felt at a complete loss. He had been blind to the developing relationship and was devastated that his love had been overlooked again.

In *Never Give all the Heart* he wrote:

> *Never give all the heart, for love*
> *Will hardly seem worth thinking of*
> *To passionate women if it seem*
> *Certain, and they never dream*
> *That it fades out from kiss to kiss;*
> *For everything that's lovely is*
> *But a brief, dreamy, kind delight.*
> *O never give the heart outright,*
> *For they, for all smooth lips can say,*
> *Have given their hearts up to the play.*
> *And who could play it well enough*
> *If deaf and dumb and blind with love?*
> *He that made this knows all the cost*
> *For he gave all his heart and lost.*

In his sexual loneliness Willie turned to an old friend Florence Farr Emery. He had met her in 1890 at Bedford Park, when she performed in *Sicilian Idyll* by John Todhunter. She had been married for a time but had no regard for Victorian morals. She had been the mistress of G.B. Shaw but they parted without animosity on either side. Willie felt he could tell her everything. They toured England, giving performances of 'cantillating' — reciting poetry to the accompaniment of a harp. Their sexual relationship lasted until she became ill with cancer in 1912. Then she went to a Buddhist college in Ceylon where she remained until her death in 1917. Willie immortalised her in a poem *All Souls' Night*:

> *On Florence Emery I call the next,*
> *Who finding the first wrinkles on a face*
> *Admired and beautiful,*
> *And knowing that the future would be vexed*
> *With 'minished beauty, multiplied commonplace,*
> *Preferred to teach a school*
> *Away from neighbour or friend,*
> *Among dark skins, and there*
> *Permit foul years to wear*
> *Hidden from eyesight to the unnoticed end . . .*

Willie went on a tour of America in November 1903 possibly to help him forget Maud's marriage. This trip, financed by Lady Gregory, was very successful. He kept Lady Gregory informed in many interesting letters and tried to repay her part of the cost but she would take nothing until he had enough to feel independent, a situation that did not arise until his third tour of America in 1914.

# 17

*Have I not seen the loveliest woman born . . .*
*Barter that horn and every good . . .*
*For an old bellows full of angry wind? . . .*

A PRAYER FOR MY DAUGHTER

Maud and John honeymooned first in Barcelona and then in Normandy. Back in Paris John expected Maud to settle down to what he would call a normal married life. A conventional man, he assumed that Maud would be happy to stay at home with him, sharing their lives. She had been used to travelling where and when she pleased and found this a constraint. She wanted to be the wife of a political hero — but an active wife, playing her own political part. The Irish Nationalists saw John as a political hero but he was aware that they used Maud for emotional appeals, and did not consider her up to leadership standard. On the other hand she was the partner with the money. She was not dependent on her husband. They quarrelled about the respective expectations from marriage but tried to keep these quarrels a secret. Maud would escape to her house in Dublin where John could not follow as he was wanted by the British.

Within a few months of the marriage Maud confided to Willie that she had married in haste and regretted it. As always he was quick to sympathise. In *A Prayer for My Daughter* he later wrote:

> *Have I not seen the loveliest woman born*
> *Out of the mouth of Plenty's horn,*
> *Because of her opinionated mind*
> *Barter that horn and every good*
> *By quiet nature understood*
> *For an old bellows full of angry wind? . . .*

Yet she was not always equally kind to Willie. When he produced Synge's play *In The Shadow Of The Glen*, in which a young wife in a loveless marriage runs off with a travelling man, Maud walked out half-way through the performance in protest at the theme. Annie Horniman, Willie's patron, paid for renovations to The Mechanics' Hall, the new home for the Abbey Players. Maud was the first to complain when the price of admission rose to six shillings, saying it would be too much for the ordinary people to pay. Willie wrote to Lady Gregory that he did not mind the misunderstanding of the indifferent but was hurt by the misunderstandings of friends.

Maud was in Dublin in July 1903 when it was announced that Edward VII was to visit Ireland. A meeting was held in the Rotunda and Maud asked John Redmond if it was true that the Irish Party intended to present the king with an address of loyalty. This sparked off a row between the Loyalists and the Nationalists and Maud had to be lifted bodily from the stage. Later Dublin Corporation voted by a slight majority not to present the address.

By coincidence the king, head of the Protestant Church, arrived in Ireland on 21 July, the same day that the head of the Catholic Church, Pope Leo XII died. The British colours and the Union Jack hung from many houses and Maud also hung out a black flag in protest. Police arrived to remove it and Maud replaced it with one of her black petticoats. A further attempt was made to seize the petticoat but Maud's maid aimed a bottle at the attacker. A detective tried to gain access to the house but Maud stopped him. Roughly he pushed her aside and her housekeeper cried: 'You dirty scoundrel, daring to lay hands on a lady. You double-murderer, daring to touch a lady in her condition!' Maud asked what she meant and got the reply: 'Don't you know, Madame? I saw him in the tea cup clear as day — a little boy in a pram'. Maud's son Seán was born the following January.

The birth of their son did not make the couple more compatible. With John's approval Maud brought their son to be baptised in the Church of the Three Patrons in Rathgar, Dublin. John O'Leary was to be godfather but, as he was a Republican and an agnostic, the priest objected. Rather than find a different godfather Maud found a sympathetic priest to perform the ceremony.

While John would have been pleased with the Irish baptism of his son, he would not have been happy that Maud spent two months in London on her way back to Paris. In the summer she returned to Ireland, leaving her husband and son behind. She was in Dublin when John Quinn arrived for his third visit. By now he was interested in the Celtic Revival and was very generous with funds for any cultural Irish event.

Willie was busy that year preparing for the opening of the Abbey Theatre. His new play *On Baile's Strand*, was in rehearsal and he and the actors gave their time and work free of charge.

Word reached Maud and Willie that John was drinking heavily. John's lack of work and Maud's absence were contributory factors. John, left at home with Iseult, Eileen and baby Seán, could have found that Iseult was Maud's natural, not adopted, daughter. When she returned home they fought and the arguments ended in violence. Willie and Lady Gregory were very worried at this turn of events and the more the rows continued the more Maud stayed away from home.

An article appeared in the *New York Evening World* on 13 August 1905 entitled: 'A Brainy Woman Should Not Wed, says Maud Gonne'. It was a report of an interview she gave to the paper's Paris correspondent. To the question — 'Is marriage a failure?' she replied: 'The answer most depends upon the woman who is the wife. If a woman really has something worthwhile doing in the world, I say, unhesitatingly, that marriage is a deplorable step for her or is likely to prove so until after she has accomplished her work. If she is an ordinary, commonplace woman, then she might as well marry as not. But a man is selfish — Oh how selfish! No matter how loving he is when first married, he is sure to become jealous or sarcastic about his wife's career. Finally he is likely to make his wife's life a hell.' John would have known that the Nationalists did not think much of Maud's intellectual prowess and so would have been sarcastic about her career in an attempt to get her to stay at home.

She continued by saying that what she said was true of nearly all men. 'I have seen it a thousand times. I have seen each of a thousand brilliant women married to some commonplace man who thinks her first duty is to worship him, then to take care of his children and home, then be grateful for enough food and clothes to live on. Moreover, in the way of happy marriages there is increasing difficulty over discrepancies in the education of the man and the woman. In these days a woman is likely to be better educated than her husband. It is a fatal error for such a woman to take on such a man . . . ' Maud had very little formal education, drifting around Europe with a governess. John may well have had more but she had many social graces that he lacked.

'Biologically, marriage may be an undoubted necessity: humanly speaking it is axiomatic; but from the viewpoint of woman's best happiness I deny that marriage is the best arrangement possible!' The fact that she says marriage may be an undoubted biological necessity, coupled with her earlier remark — 'No matter how loving he is when he is first married' — would indicate that they had a good sexual relationship at first. She had had a monogamous relationship with Millevoye for thirteen years, and within a few months of the end of this affair she had met John and, on the American trip, mentioned he had proposed to her, so despite her protestations of frigidity to Willie, she was thinking of John in sexual terms. She would have been more honest if she said that, for her 'biologically sex may be an undoubted necessity . . . I deny that marriage is the best arrangement possible.' She had been happy as a mistress.

She said that in one hundred homes you would find 'at least seventy-five quite happy men of all classes, whose work and income are various, and at least ninety-five women who are unhappy or whose lives are incomplete, each by reason of her husband's congenital conviction that the main thing in the world is his content and comfort. Probably, in each case he thinks that because he keeps a roof over his wife's head he is the worthiest thing under the roof; he thinks only of his career, his advancement, his development . . . His poor wife, rather bewildered, takes his view until she forgets she had any other.'

'Are not the family responsibilities common to most marriages more to blame than the husband for un-happiness?' asked the reporter.

Maud replied: 'I do not see why, just because a woman is a wife and mother she must be a housekeeper. If she has the capacity to follow a profession and to help to earn money, why should she not give over domestic drudgery to well-chosen and well-paid servants? Why should a man feel that other men despise him if his wife makes money, or if she does not need to make money, follows her profession for love of it?'

Maud did not earn money, she inherited it and it gave her an income. John would never have objected to well-chosen, well-paid servants. Maud always had them. All he wanted was that she should spend more time with her husband and child. The fact that she had a past lover haunted him. He was lonely and jealous. John, still exiled from his beloved Ireland, began to meet his old wartime friends and started to drink heavily.

Winding up the interview she said: 'To my mind the whole situation can be summed up thus: marriage could be the greatest success in the sociological history of humanity if the man would or could play fair. But I believe any woman with independent instincts, with the dream of making her individual personality count for something in the world, might just as well shun marriage.'

How well Griffith and John's brother knew when they gave their advice that they should not marry!

This interview lost Maud many supporters and she regretted giving it. It seemed unfair to John but was published after their separation and was an emotional outburst as she could not give the real reason of their final fracas. One evening John became drunk and made a sexual attack on Eileen. Maud was frantic. To cover up the scandal she insisted that her beautiful eighteen-year-old half-sister should marry John's forty-three year old brother Joseph. This was an indication of how strong-willed Maud was. Eileen who had been reared in Howth for most of her life and spent only a few years with Maud, did her bidding. It was more surprising that Joseph agreed, and in December 1904 the two were married in Paris.

All semblance of marriage between Maud and John was gone forever.

# 18

Out of the depths of despair Maud turned to Willie once more for consolation. He travelled with her to Paris and wrote to Lady Gregory: 'Dear Friend, I turn to you in every trouble. I cannot bear the burden of this terrible case alone — I know nothing about lawyers and so on. When you know the story you will feel that if she were the uttermost stranger, or the bitterest enemy one would have, even to the putting aside of all else, to help her.'

Lady Gregory asked a lawyer friend to draw up a separation agreement which Maud signed but John would not. This left Maud with no choice but to file for a legal separation as her main concern was to gain custody of Seán. She hired private detectives and Quinn tried unsuccessfully to establish defamatory evidence against John in America.

The *United Irishman* did not mention a word of the case but on 28 February 1905 the *Irish Independent*, quoting the *London Daily News* printed: 'The husband is charged with cruelty, infidelity, drunkenness. He is at present living apart from his wife, but she alleges that on several occasions when she was away from home he brought home tipsy Irishmen who slept in her bed.' John was horrified at this newspaper report and started a libel case against the *Irish Independent*. Newspapers in England were not allowed to report on the case while it was pending. The libel case delayed the hearing of the divorce case.

Early in 1905 John indicated that he was willing to settle out of court if Maud would withhold the most damning evidence. The case was heard on 26 July 1905 by the Civil

Tribunal of the Seine and she was finally granted a separation, but not a divorce, on 9 August. Happily for both sides the charges of intemperance were thought sufficient. An article in the *Irish Independent* 10 August 1905 stated: 'The Court grants Mrs MacBride the custody of the child for the present, with permission to Major MacBride to see him every Monday between three and five o'clock, at the mother's residence, and in the presence of a third party, who is named in the judgment.' A further clause gave John the right to have Seán for the whole month of August each year after he reached the age of six.

John's exile from Ireland had been lifted and he returned there to work once more for the Irish movement with John O'Leary and his Nationalist friends.

Maud stayed in France until the separation decree became final in 1906. In October of that year she tested the water by returning for a visit to see Lady Gregory's play, *The Gaol Gate*. As she walked through the audience with Willie the crowd began to hiss and a cry of 'Up MacBride' was heard. Some tried to drown out the hissing. Maud appeared unperturbed but it was the first time she had come across such a reaction from an Irish crowd. While the crowd thought her unmoved Willie could see the anguish in her heart and wrote a poem called *The People* in which he recorded his disgust:

> *'What have I earned for all that work,' I said,*
> *'For all that I have done at my own charge?*
> *The daily spite of this unmannerly town,*
> *Where who has served the most is most defamed,*
> *The reputation of his lifetime lost . . .'*
> *Thereon my phoenix answered in reproof,*
> *'The drunkards, pilferers of public funds,*
> *All the dishonest crowd I had driven away,*
> *When my luck changed and they dared meet my face,*
> *Crawled from obscurity, and set upon me*

*Those I had served and some that I had fed;*
*Yet never have I, now nor at any time,*
*Complained of the people . . .'*

The people were not entirely to blame. Maud and John were relieved that the full facts had not come out in the court but this left many unanswered questions for the Irish public. Reports of the separation said the reason was intemperance. In Ireland sexual sins were held in greater contempt that intemperance. A 'fallen woman' was far worse than a 'hard man', as a drinker would be called. Her published views on marriage did not help her cause. Rumours abounded. Had John been unfaithful? If this question was asked by Maud's supporters John's friends would counter this with queries of her supposed lover in France and her child.

Willie, Lady Gregory and Maud's close friends showed great sympathy towards Maud but she had lost the adulation of the crowd. She had had three great loves, her father who died suddenly, Lucien who had left her for another woman and the people of Ireland who now rejected her.

Maud would say that she went to live in France because her separation was not recognised in Ireland and John could have claimed his son if she brought him to Ireland. This was not the full story. John never demanded to see his son. Three years after the separation decree Maud went back to court and, as a result, John MacBride was refused the right to have his son for the month of August. Despite the fact that her religion forbade it she appealed for a complete divorce. The appeal was refused but she was given the right to re-open the case in a further three years. She decided that, as long as John kept his distance from her and Seán, she would not bother to go to court again. She appeared to have no great fear that John would claim his son.

She had always kept her daughter in France and Iseult was being educated in a suitable convent. Bringing her to Ireland would have added to the rumours. When Ireland turned its back on Maud she decided to spend the winters in Paris and the summers with her children at Les Mouettes, Colleville-sur-Mer, Calvados in Normandy. She kept in touch with Ireland through the Daughters of Erin and, of course, through Willie.

He visited her frequently in France and stayed in the Hotel Passy near her in Paris or at the house in Normandy. In Willie's cryptic diaries it says that their love was consummated at least once in 1907. Perhaps he wrote of his love in his letters to Maud which were later destroyed. It would be heartwarming to think that he wrote her a love poem for her eyes only, he could not have published it as, in Ireland, she was still married to John.

Willie's ardour did not grow less but hers did not grow more. She did not want a physical relationship with Willie to continue and in June 1908 he wrote in his journal ' . . . On Saturday evening she said something that blotted away the recent past and brought all back to the spiritual marriage of 1898 . . . She believes that this bond is to be recreated . . . It is to be the bond of the spirit only and she lives from now on, she said . . . for that and for her children.'

This renewal of their spiritual marriage was precious to both and lasted from June 1908 to January 1909 and they believed they could come together in dreams. They kept a record of the details of these unions in a white calf-skin notebook in which both wrote — extracts were published in Virginia Moore's *The Unicorn, William Butler Yeats' Search for Reality*.

One such union was recorded by Willie on 25 July 1908, and confirmed by her the following day. It took place in space and he took the form of a great serpent and, while

she says their lips met and they 'melted' into one another, it was a spiritual rather than a physical union. It is hard to see how she could claim that there was nothing physical in this. They were both in their early forties and he had spent over twenty years telling her of his physical desire for her.

Willie would always explain away her actions. Their second spiritual marriage ended in January 1909 and at the end of that month he wrote in his journal: 'We are divided by her religious ideas and Catholicism which has grown on her. She will not divorce her husband and marry because of her Church. Since she said this she has been further from me but is always very near. She too seems to love more than of old. In addition to this the old dread of physical love was awakened in her.

'This dread has probably spoiled her life, checking natural and instinctive selection, and leaving fantastic duties free to take its place. It is what philosophy is to me, a daily rooter out of instinct and guiding joy — and all the while she grows nobler under the touch of sorrow and denial. What end will it all have? I fear for her and for myself. She has all myself. I was never more deeply in love, but my desires must go elsewhere if I would escape their poison. I am in continual terror of some entanglement parting us, and all the while I know that she made me and I her. She is my innocence and I her wisdom.'

A day later he continues: 'Today the thought came to me that PIAL (her name in the Golden Dawn) never really understands my plans, or nature or ideas. Then came the thought, what matters? How much of the best I have done and still do is but the attempt to explain myself to her? If she understood, I should lack a reason for writing, and one never can have too many reasons for doing what is so laborious.'

Maud had once said that the world would thank her for not marrying him as he made beautiful poetry out of his unhappiness and here Willie confirms that out of his unrequited love grew his best work.

Willie was described as a born heretic. Maud shared this heresy until just before her marriage to John when she was received into the Catholic Church yet their ideas of faithfulness were entirely different.

Mentally he never gave his heart to another woman but physically he could see nothing wrong with having affairs. As well as with Olivia and Florence Farr he had a long relationship with Mabel Dickenson a medical masseuse in London — and there were others. He did not believe in the teachings of any religion and, if both parties were willing, could see nothing wrong with such liaisons.

Maud on the other hand, was physically faithful to Lucien for thirteen years because she loved him. Despite her great beauty and many conquests she did not have a long list of lovers. Again this was in pre-contraceptive days and an affair, for a woman, could result in unwanted pregnancies. She could see no wrong in having a spiritual marriage with Willie while she was still living with Lucien. She must have been physically attracted to John or she would not have contemplated marriage. In a short time the constraints of marriage came between them. Obviously, too, Willie would expect her to give up all her political activities, so, from her point of view, it was wiser to keep their relationship on the 'spiritual' level and she could make her supposed dread of sex the reason for keeping Willie on a string. Although she knew she was causing him untold unhappiness she convinced herself that this was justified by his love poems.

Some poems nominally written to someone else, were also about Maud — one to Iseult, *To A Young Girl*, reads:

> *My dear, my dear, I know*
> *More than another*

*What makes your heart beat so;*
*Not even your own mother*
*Can know it as I know,*
*Who broke my heart for her*
*When the wild thought,*
*That she denies*
*And has forgot,*
*Set all her blood astir*
*And glittered in her eyes.*

# 19

*I have no child, I have nothing but a book,*
*Nothing but that to prove your blood and mine.*

INTRODUCTORY RHYMES

Willie's work for the Irish theatre continued. On 26 January 1907 a production of Synge's *The Playboy Of the Western World* caused uproar. The Nationalists regarded it as a ridicule of the Irish people and Willie felt they had no intellectual appreciation of true art. A public debate was held about the play and Willie's father spoke out in favour of it. In *Beautiful Lofty Things* he wrote:

*My father upon the Abbey stage, before him a raging crowd . . .*

The public had turned their back on Willie as well as Maud and he escaped to Italy for a holiday with Lady Gregory and her son, Robert.

In 1908 friends gathered money to send J.B. to Italy also but instead he used the money to go to America with Lily for an exhibition of her work. Although they were well received they outstayed their welcome. Lily came home but J.B. spent the remainder of his life in America. Describing him, a New York barrister remarked that: 'In Dublin it is hopeless insolvency — here it is hopeful insolvency', a view J.B. shared. At Willie's request John Quinn agreed to look after his father.

Willie went on one of his many visits to Maud in France early in May 1910, leaving Lennox Robinson, a young Cork playwright, in charge of the Abbey Theatre.

Edward VII died on 7 May and Robinson's reaction was to keep the theatre open but he sent a telegram to Lady Gregory to ask her advice. This was delayed and the matinee was in progress when the reply arrived advising closure. Miss Horniman, main patron of the Abbey, sent a telegram — 'Subsidy ceases now unless Directors and Robinson express regret in Dublin press that decent example was not followed'. Lady Gregory published an apology which Miss Horniman did not accept. Arthur Griffith said, in his weekly journal: 'Mr Yeats is not in Ireland at the present, and circumstances may have prevented him reading the insult which his co-directors have accepted in the spirit of whipped curs. Whether he will permit himself to be whipped in public in return for English money, remains to be seen.' This was another indication of the animosity that still existed between Willie and the Nationalists.

Miss Horniman withdrew as patron of the Abbey. To raise money Willie gave lectures in London on his memories of the Rhymers Club and on the playwright Synge. The proceeds, together with private donations gave the Abbey a new lease of life.

Despite his work Willie was not free from financial worries. His uncle George Pollexfen, died later that year but left most of his money to the Pollexfen relatives. To help Willie, Lady Gregory and Edmund Gosse got him on the civil list, a pension given by royal favour — without commiting him to any political loyalties. Nationalists called him Pensioner Yeats.

Lady Gregory and Lennox Robinson were in America during the winter of 1911–12 leaving Willie in charge of the Abbey. Lady Gregory renewed acquaintance with John Quinn. He had come to visit her in Coole in 1904 but now the relationship blossomed and when she came home she wrote to him: 'My John, my dear John, my own John, not other people's John . . . ' and described the relationship as a rapture of friendship.

While they were away Willie made a short visit to England where he met Olivia Shakespear. He also met her brother and his wife, formerly Mrs Hyde-Lees of Pickhill Hall, Wrexham. Some months later he met Mrs Hyde-Lees' daughter by her first marriage, Georgina (George) Hyde-Lees, who was twenty years of age at that time. She was interested in literature and music and they had frequent meetings during the following five years. Neither seemed to realise that this friendship would lead to marriage.

Meanwhile Maud was enjoying life with her children in France. In 1909 she visited Ireland and in 1910 brought her children over thus giving the lie to her statement that she feared John would seize Seán. John had been building up his reputation again through his membership of the IRB. He and Maud shared an interest in Sinn Féin, a party that hoped to promote Irish industries in Ireland. In 1911 John chaired a meeting in the Rotunda, to mark Robert Emmet's birthday. Maud attended and although their paths crossed they were not on friendly terms. She had reverted to the name of Maud Gonne.

Maud was horrified to discover that Irish school-children were not allowed home for lunch and indeed, that many children did not receive a breakfast. In France schools provided a lunch for children and she resolved to start something similar in Ireland. She enlisted the help of Constance Gore-Booth, who had married a Polish count and had acquired the title of Countess Markievicz.

Constance had become very involved with Irish issues. She had given her daughter, Maeve, to her mother, Lady Gore-Booth, to rear so that she could devote herself fully to her work for Ireland. She had been criticised for this but Maud defended her saying that she was not a negligent mother but had, unselfishly, given up a personal life for her country. Constance shared Maud's view that Irish youth should be trained to fight for Ireland. She founded an organisation called 'The Fianna' which taught its members how to handle and use guns.

Inspired by this, Maud continued to go to Normandy for the summer months but during the winter she left her children at school in Paris and came back to Dublin to set up canteens for starving schoolchildren. At St Auden's she and her team, which included Constance, fed two hundred and fifty children during the first year.

Willie was quick to laud this in *Her Praise*:

> She is foremost of those I would hear praised.
> I have gone about the house, gone up and down
> As a man does who has published a new book,
> Or a young girl dressed out in a new gown,
> And though I have turned the talk by hook or crook
> Until her praise should be the uppermost theme,
> A woman spoke of some new tale she had read,
> A man confusedly in a half dream
> As though some other name ran in his head.
> She is foremost of those I would hear praised.
> I will talk no more of books or the long war
> But walk by the dry thorn until I have found
> Some beggar sheltering from the wind, and there
> Manage the talk until her name come round.
> If there be rags enough he will know her name
> And be well pleased remembering it, for in the old days,
> Though she had young men's praise and old men's blame,
> Among the poor both old and young gave her praise.

Normandy, in the summer, seemed a world apart. The house, 'Les Mouettes' called after the seagulls, had been given to Maud in trust for Iseult by Lucien. During Willie's visits they argued eternally about their old disagreement over Synge's play and Sinn Féin.

Maud busied herself with a monthly woman's magazine called *Bean na hÉireann*, produced by the Daughters of Erin. Willie worked for the theatre and became involved with

Lady Gregory's nephew Hugh Lane, in attempting to find a home for modern paintings in Dublin. In April 1910 Willie became a member of the Royal Society of Literature and published a new book of poetry.

As the years passed he despaired of marrying Maud and wrote a poem, *Introductory Rhymes*, to his forebears:

> *Pardon, old fathers, if you still remain*
> *Somewhere in ear-shot for the story's end,*
> *Old Dublin merchant 'free of the ten and four'*
> *Or trading out of Galway into Spain;*
> *Old country scholar, Robert Emmet's friend,*
> *A hundred-year-old memory to the poor;*
> *Merchant and scholar who have left me blood*
> *That has not passed through any huckster's loin,*
> *Soldier that gave, whatever die was cast:*
> *A Butler or an Armstrong that withstood*
> *Beside the brackish waters of the Boyne*
> *James and his Irish when the Dutchmen crossed;*
> *Old merchant skipper that leaped overboard*
> *After a ragged hat in Biscay Bay;*
> *You most of all, silent and fierce old man,*
> *Because the daily spectacle that stirred*
> *My fancy, and set my boyish lips to say,*
> *'Only the wasteful virtues earn the sun';*
> *Pardon that for a barren passion's sake,*
> *Although I have come close on forty-nine,*
> *I have no child, I have nothing but a book,*
> *Nothing but that to prove your blood and mine.*

Willie's ancestry was very important to him and the thought that he would not continue the line did not please him. He took less and less interest in political events in Ireland and concentrated on his writings. The Home Rule Bill had two readings, which were not acceptable to the

Ulster Unionists, while the Nationalists prepared to arm themselves for possible confrontation. In 1913 a strike in Dublin by workers who thought 14 hours a day too long to work was backed by Jim Larkin, head of the Transport Workers' Union. This led to a lockout and Maud, with her experience of soup kitchens, helped to feed the starving strikers. This continued until she got word that Seán was ill in France with measles so she left immediately to be with him.

She had visited St Enda's, Pádraig Pearse's school in Cullenswood, Rathmines where Irish and Nationalism were given pride of place in the education of pupils. She longed to send Seán to this school but it would have been too near John's interests and she wanted to keep the two apart.

She was in France when the First World War started in 1914. From the outset Maud was totally against the war but her compassion was aroused by the wounded French so she and Iseult joined the Red Cross to help take care of the injured. On 7 January, 1915 she wrote to Quinn that the whole situation had become very depressing — as soon as the wounded were nursed back to health they were sent back into battle again.

In Ireland, John Redmond believed that Irishmen should join England in the European war and looked for Irish recruits. Lady Gregory, whose son Robert later joined the Air Force supported this view, as did Willie. Maud was totally against it. Lady Cunard invited both Willie and Lord Wimborne, the viceroy, to a dinner party. Lord Wimborne wanted Willie to give recruitment his public support and said that the Prime Minister was thinking of being 'very gracious' to him. According to Hone in a letter to his sister Willie wrote: ' . . . here is a piece of very private information for you, I have just refused a knight-hood. Lady Cunard had already sounded the authorities and asked me about it. Please keep it to yourself as it would be very ungracious of me to let it get talked about in Dublin. It was very kindly meant. I said "As I grow older I become more conservative and I do not know whether that is because my thoughts are deeper or my blood more chill but I do not wish anyone to say of me 'only for a ribbon he left us'".' This of course referred to the poem by Browning — 'Just for a handful of silver he left us, just for a riband to stick in his coat.'

He may not have wished anyone to say that of him but he knew that Maud would have been the first. She would certainly have influenced his refusal. The mere thought of an English title or a request to help the English in the fray would have put an insurmountable barrier between them.

Maud continued with her war work in France. When German submarines sank the liner *Lusitania*, with Lady Gregory's nephew, Hugh Lane on board Willie went to Coole to sympathise with Lady Gregory. A controversy arose about an unsigned codicil to Hugh Lane's will in which he left his collection of French paintings to the Irish people.

Neither Willie nor Maud was aware that the IRB were training their members for a possible showdown with the British.

# 20

*All changed, changed utterly:*
*A terrible beauty is born...*

EASTER 1916

With England at war the Irish Nationalists belonging to the Irish Republican Brotherhood felt that 'England's difficulty — Ireland's opportunity' and organised a Rising for 24 April, 1916. This was a new and much changed IRB from that which Maud and Willie had joined years earlier. Many Nationalists were not in favour of the Rising. Eoin MacNeill, head of the Volunteers was informed only at the last minute. By then he had got word that the British had captured Roger Casement, who was bringing *The Aud*, with arms aboard, into Tralee. The boat had been scuttled. MacNeill was to bring 10,000 men but, with this adverse news and the delay with the information, he managed to enlist only a tenth of the promised supporters. The Rising was largely confined to Dublin.

It was the Easter Bank holiday and most of the gentry and officers were at Fairyhouse races. Pádraig Pearse joined Connolly to set up headquarters at the General Post Office in Sackville (O'Connell) Street. Other leaders took up key positions around the city including Countess Markievicz, who was in Stephen's Green.

John MacBride had not been told of the Rising and was on his way home from a wedding when he noticed the fighting and joined Thomas MacDonagh at Jacob's biscuit factory, overlooking Dublin Castle. His experience as a military man proved very useful and he became one of the leaders and organised raiding parties. The Rising lasted for six days before it was contained and MacBride was arrested with the leaders.

Although Willie had not taken much interest in recent Irish politics he was strangely moved by the Rising. He was staying with Sir Rothenstein in Gloucestershire, England and wondered why he had no knowledge that it was brewing. His fellow poets were all involved — Pearse, MacDonagh and Joseph Mary Plunkett. MacBride was in jail and Willie sent Maud copies of the newspapers every day. An incorrect report said that Connolly was dead.

Maud was in Normandy with Seán and Iseult and she, too, was taken by surprise. Her first reaction was to get to Ireland but she knew that, even if she got as far as England, it would be impossible to get a passport. Within a week she wrote to Quinn that her husband, John MacBride, was in jail with the wounded Pearse. Her great friend Countess Markievicz was also imprisoned. She was relieved to hear that although Connolly was badly wounded the newspaper report that he was dead had been denied.

Because only a few Nationalists had been involved initially the Irish public did not sympathise with those who took part. This quickly changed when, within a fortnight, sixteen of the leaders were executed before a firing squad. John MacBride was one of those executed. A Franciscan priest, Father Augustine, who anointed John when he died, wrote to Maud that he alone, could tell her how calmly and 'with most admirable fortitude' John had died, having prepared for his end like a good Catholic.

Maud had known and loved those who took part in the Rising and considered them heroes from the start. She was appalled by the executions and wrote to Quinn giving him details. She said that John had died for his country and that her son would bear an honoured name. John was buried at Arbour Hill and Maud did not succeed in having his body exhumed and re-buried at Glasnevin.

J.B. Yeats, still living in America, heard of the Rising and wrote a very astute letter to his daughter, Lily: '. . . so those poor rebels have been executed. The government has done the logical thing, the average thing . . . and yet

the wrong thing. These men are now embalmed in the Irish memory, and hatred of England, which might have died out, is now revived. Kept alive in prison, Ireland would have pitied and loved and smiled at these men, knowing them to be mad fools. These poor fools are now heroes and martyrs for all time, and their folly has done more for Ireland and for the dignity of Irishmen than anybody's wisdom.'

Willie had only one letter from Maud during this period, telling him that she had a vision of Sackville (O'Connell) Street in ruins. He wrote to Lady Gregory saying that he was surprisingly moved. He had been striving for Irish Nationalism by going back to old Irish stories to establish a cultural identity. He had always thought that Maud was wrong in promoting violence and was convinced that few people wanted this violence. When the Rising took place, he wondered what would become of his ideals for, like many an Irish person, his convictions were upturned and his sympathies were with the leaders who had been executed. He had kept his literary career free from politics yet felt compelled to write a poem about the Rising. The line that ran through his head was 'terrible beauty has been born again'. This, in time, would become *All is changed, changed utterly, A terrible beauty is born* . . . He worked on this poem, *Easter 1916*, but did not set it down on paper until September 1916. It was printed immediately but given out by hand only and did not reach the public until 1920. He included John MacBride's name in the list of heroes:

> *We know their dream; enough*
> *To know they dreamed and are dead;*
> *And what if excess of love*
> *Bewildered them till they died?*
> *I write it out in a verse —*

*MacDonagh and MacBride*
*And Connolly and Pearse*
*Now and in time to be,*
*Wherever green is worn,*
*Are changed, changed utterly:*
*A terrible beauty is born.*

Death had changed Maud's and Willie's opinion of John MacBride. She, who had avoided him in life, was pleased to be the widow of one of Ireland's heroes who had made the glorious sacrifice of giving his life for his country. Willie could not forget the past quite so easily:

*This other man I had dreamed*
*A drunken vainglorious lout.*
*He had done most bitter wrong*
*To some who are near to my heart,*
*Yet I number him in the song;*
*He, too, has resigned his part*
*In the casual comedy;*
*He, too, has been changed in his turn,*
*Transformed utterly:*
*A terrible beauty is born . . .*

Maud wanted to be back in Ireland with Seán and Iseult but was repeatedly refused a passport. She sent Iseult to Willie for assistance but even he could not help. On this trip Iseult met and made friends with George Hyde-Lees.

Joseph MacBride, Eileen's husband, who lived at Mallow Cottage, Westport, was desolate after John's death. His marriage to Eileen seems to have been a happy one and they had five children. Suddenly their peaceful world was invaded when Joseph, although he took no part in politics, was arrested and deported to Wakefield Prison without trial. No visitors were allowed and he was held in

solitary confinement. Reports smuggled out of the prison came to Maud's ears: 'he lay shivering in his cell, listening to the screams of his fellow prisoners being kicked and lashed in the prison yard.' Due to the cold and bad food his health deteriorated and he was allowed to return home where Eileen nursed him back to health but no sooner was he better than he was re-arrested and sent back to jail this time to Reading. He was allowed to work at the Bodleian Library and a few months later, was sent to a Gloucestershire village and ordered to remain within a five mile radius. No work or money was provided and the Irish Prisoner's Aid Society saved him from starvation.

Eileen, who had been such a tower of strength to him, was also worried about her mother Margaret Wilson. As governess to Baron Budberg's family in Petersburg she would have been affected by the shortages in Russia that caused the revolution of 1917. The Budberg family sent Margaret to their estates in Estonia and, when she was no longer needed as a governess, she was kept on there as a caretaker.

# 21

*I, the poet William Yeats,*
*With old mill boards and sea-green slates,*
*And smithy work from the Gort forge,*
*Restored this tower for my wife George . . .*

CARVED ON A STONE AT THOOR BALLYLEE

If Willie's reasoning had been correct Maud did not marry him because of her religion. According to the Catholic Church she was married to John until 1916. Now she was a widow, so he assumed that she was free to marry him at last. He proposed to her in the summer of 1916 but was again refused. He always had a reason for Maud's rejection and, in a letter to Florence Farr, written on 18 August 1916 he said: 'The death of her husband had made no difference to our relationship. She belongs now to the Third Order of St Francis and sighs for a convent . . .'

She may well have been a member of the Third Order but she certainly did not long for a convent. She longed to be back in Ireland, accepted by the people as the widow of one of the 1916 heroes.

Willie had given up all hope that Maud would marry him. On his visits to Normandy, he turned his attention to Iseult who had grown to be very beautiful. He proposed to her twice possibly seeing in her what her mother had been, but she refused on both occasions.

Now over fifty, Willie turned to twenty five-year-old Georgina (George) Hyde-Lees. He proposed and was accepted. A wealthy young lady of great charm and culture, George married him at the Harrow Road Registry Office in London on 20 October 1917. The poet, Ezra Pound, married to Olivia Shakespear's daughter, was the best man.

Willie's daughter Anne described many years later in an article in the *Irish Times* (26 January 1989) how 'quite soon after they were married, father was quite depressed. His head was full of the beginnings of the vision, his scheme for religion, and she (George) thought she would try to fake automatic writing to keep him interested. She said that she started it and something took hold of her hand.' Willie would ask questions which the 'spirits' would answer through George's writing.

He was worried that, by his marriage, he had betrayed three people — Maud, Iseult and George but according to Levenson George wrote 'with the bird, all is well at heart. Your action was right for both but in London you mistook its meaning.' He took this to mean that Iseult was happy about his marriage and it gave him peace of mind.

Despite the age difference, it was a suitable match and Willie was delighted with his young wife. According to Hone he wrote to his father: 'I am dictating this to my wife. I call her George to avoid Georgie which she has been called hitherto, in spite of her protests. I enclose her photograph. She permits me to say that it flatters her good looks at the expense of her character. She is not so black and white, but has red-brown hair and a high colour which she sets off by wearing dark green in her clothes and earrings . . .'

Another letter to Lady Gregory tells: '. . . my wife is a perfect wife, kind, wise and unselfish. I think you were such another young girl once. She has made my life serene and full of order' and he continued by describing the change in Woburn Buildings: '. . . Nothing changed in plan but little touches here and there, and my own bedroom (the old bathroom) with furniture of unpolished wood as for years I have wished for. Then there is a dinner service of great purple plates for meat, and various earthenware bowls for other purposes. Then too, all is very clean . . .'

After a honeymoon in England Willie brought George to Ireland. He had acquired an old Norman tower at Ballylee in County Galway. It had been part of the Gregory estate taken over by the Congested Districts Board and sold to Willie for £35. It had four large apartments with wide fireplaces and mullioned windows. They decided to restore the tower and Lady Gregory loaned them the near-by Ballinamantane House while the restoration was in progress. The restored tower bears this inscription:

> *I, the poet William Yeats*
> *With old mill boards and sea-green slates*
> *And smithy work from the Gort forge,*
> *Restored this tower for my wife George;*
> *And may these characters remain*
> *When all is ruin once again.*

George's daughter, Anne, in a television interview in 1989 said that, although she knew much about her father and his work she had no knowledge of her mother's interests. Anne said that George centred her whole life around Willie and his work. She encouraged him, read his writings and corrected the odd spelling, ensured that no one interrupted him while he was working and, indeed, was a perfect wife for Willie. George appreciated Willie's work before he received world acclaim, and at his request, contacted his spirit world with her automatic writing. No other woman could have given him so much peace and contentment — certainly not Maud. Lily Yeats felt that Maud and Lady Gregory were both pleased by the marriage while Arthur Symons wrote to Quinn that Maud felt George would either become Willie's slave or leave him.

## 22

*A grey gull lost its fear and flew*
*Down to her cell and there alit . . .*

ON A POLITICAL PRISONER

Surprisingly, Iseult and George became good friends and Iseult went to stay with the couple for the first Christmas after their wedding. They were of similar ages and had similar interests. After Christmas, Willie, always interested in the occult, read about Dame Alice Kyteler who had been found guilty of witchcraft in the fourteenth century in Kilkenny. He referred to her in *Nineteen Hundred and Nineteen*:

> *to whom the love-lorn Lady Kyteler brought*
> *Bronzed peacock feathers, red combs of her cocks.*

Willie was wrong to call her 'love-lorn'. She had four husbands! The Kilkenny connection awakened his interest in his Butler ancestors who had been Earls and Dukes of Ormond in that city. (Lord Dunboyne thought Willie a better poet than historian — he remarked in a letter to me: 'He wrote a splendid poem about his Butler ancestors at the battle of the Boyne but had to alter it all radically after someone reminded him that he had his ancestors fighting on the wrong side in the first version'.)

Willie asked George to contact his Butler ancestors through her automatic writing and on 23 February, 1918 a message appeared from Anne Hyde, Countess of Ossory (Ossary was an old name for the Kilkenny area and Anne had married James Butler in 1682). She had come to give the Yeatses her 'dear love'. Two days later George said she dreamed of her and that her child had lived only three days and she herself had died soon afterwards. George did not become pregnant immediately but the thought of reincarnation pleased Willie.

In the same month of February 1918 Maud tired of waiting for a passport and so slipped into Ireland in disguise. She was ignored by the authorities at first and rented a house at 73, Stephen's Green. For many years she had been known by her single name but now she wanted her son Seán to be aware that his father had died for Ireland so she reverted to Maud Gonne MacBride. Lady Gregory's son Robert had been killed in action when his plane was shot down in Italy so Maud went to Galway to sympathise with her. While there she called on Willie and George before returning to Dublin.

In April Lloyd George, British Prime Minister, had a bill passed that made conscription applicable in Ireland. This was not accepted by the Irish and two million signed a declaration against such a policy and a one-day general strike was held.

Henry Duke, chief secretary for Ireland, urged Lloyd George to arrest all known Nationalist leaders. The trumped up reason given was that they were conspiring with the German government. Seventy-three arrests were made on 17 May, 1918. Maud was arrested as she left AE's house with a member of parliament, Joseph King. Her fourteen year old son, Seán, ran after the Black Maria that took her away.

Also arrested that same night was Joseph MacBride who, for a third time, was deported and imprisoned without trial. He was with Arthur Griffith who wrote of Joseph from Gloucester Prison two months later: 'He is the oldest of the prisoners here and the confinement is visibly affecting him'.

Maud was taken to the Bridewell and then to Arbour Hill Military Prison where she was the first woman prisoner. Finally she was incarcerated in Holloway Prison in England.

The scene of his mother being taken away in such a manner haunted both Maud and Seán. She was not allowed to write cheques or to send money and had no idea what had happened to him. In fact he was sent to Mt Benedict School in Gorey, County Wexford and spent his holidays in Galway with Willie and George who grew to love him.

He had already joined Fianna Éireann, founded by Countess Markievicz.

Countess Markievicz and Kathleen Clarke, widow of the Nationalist Tom Clarke, were Maud's companions in jail. As a concession, Maud was allowed to keep her canary and she and Countess Markievicz each had a pot plant. These were small comforts as the three were left without light for twelve hours each night and had only one hour's exercise in the yard each day. Constance Markievicz had meals delivered from outside but the other two survived on prison food which did not agree with Maud and, finally all three were sent to the hospital wing.

While they were in hospital letters were at last delivered to them. Maud learned that on 25 March, 1918 Lucien had died of pulmonary congestion. His son had been killed in the war, predeceasing Lucien by a year. Until his death Lucien retained the position of editor of *La Patrie* which Maud had encouraged him to take up. Aged 67 he had been chairman of the French army's committee on aviation and a deputy for the sixteenth Arrondissement of Paris. It had been eighteen years since Maud had broken with him but he had been her one love. According to Nancy Cardozo Kathleen Clark said: 'All she'd do was talk to her canary . . . She was like a caged wild animal herself, like a tigress roving endlessly up and down. We were given the chance to apply to the Sankey Commission for release, and in her misery, she said she would — said she'd point out she hadn't been in Ireland during the war. Con said: "If you do that, you need never come back to Ireland" and she tore the application up.'

Little comfort was her caged bird to her now! Constance too had tamed a seagull which Willie wrote about in a poem entitled *On a Political Prisoner*. Strangely it was about Con not Maud that he wrote:

> *A grey gull lost its fear and flew*
> *Down to her cell and there alit,*

*And there endured her fingers' touch*
*And from her fingers ate its bit.*

*Did she in touching that lone wing*
*Recall the years before her mind*
*Became a bitter, an abstract thing,*
*Her thought some popular enmity . . .*

In October Maud was told that her sister Kathleen had died at a sanatorium in Davos. She could take no more.

Her health deteriorated at such a rate that a doctor was called. On 21 October Dr Tunnicliffe of King's College Hospital recorded that she urgently needed open air treatment.

When Iseult heard the news she contacted Willie who, at that time, was staying in Maud's house in Stephen's Green as George was expecting their first child. He made the necessary contacts and Maud was released on condition that she stay in a sanatorium in England. After a mere five days Maud discharged herself from the nursing home in which she was being treated and went to stay with Iseult in Willie's apartment in Woburn Buildings.

On the eleventh day of the eleventh month of 1918 the Armistice was signed. Lloyd George refused to put the Home Rule Act into force as he would not support a settlement which would involve forcible coercion of Ulster.

By the end of the month the passport requirements for Ireland were lifted. Although her detention under the Realm Act was not lifted, by pretending to be a Red Cross Nurse, Maud came to Dublin on 23 November. She brought Iseult and Seán with her. When she arrived at her own house at Stephen's Green Willie would not let her in because George was seven months pregnant and was recovering from pneumonia. He feared a police raid and its effects on George. Maud could not believe that he would do this. She called him an unpatriotic coward and left for friends in Wicklow. This was the first time that Willie had ever put Maud in second place.

# 23

*May she be granted beauty and yet not*
*Beauty to make a stranger's eye distraught . . .*

A PRAYER FOR MY DAUGHTER

The baby George carried was very precious to Willie. He had always been proud of his ancestry, in particular his Butler connections, and to reincarnate one of these ancestors was foremost in his mind. On 24 February, almost twelve months after Anne, Countess of Ossory, first contacted them George gave birth to a daughter. She was christened Anne after the Countess. While Willie was delighted with his daughter and wrote her a poem immediately she was born, he could not forget Maud:

> *May she be granted beauty and yet not*
> *Beauty to make a stranger's eye distraught,*
> *Or hers before a looking glass, for such,*
> *Being made beautiful overmuch,*
> *Consider beauty a sufficient end,*
> *Lose natural kindness and maybe*
> *The heart-revealing intimacy*
> *That chooses right, and never find a friend . . .*

Four months later on 19 June 1919, the Countess contacted them again and suggested that Willie should write her history. The following month he and George visited Kilkenny in search of local information. They visited Kilkenny Castle and were impressed by its size. They went to St Canice's Cathedral nearby, where many of the Butler family had been buried, but could find no trace of her tomb or indeed, any further details about her.

What they did not discover, but would have interested them was that in Kilkenny Castle there is a fine white

111

marble fireplace with scenes depicting events in the lives of the Butler family. The third panel shows King Richard II on a visit to the castle, acting as godfather to the second son of the third Earl of Ormond. The baby shown on this fireplace, was named Richard after the monarch and was knighted in 1425 by Henry VI. Willie Yeats was a direct descendant of the infant shown on the fireplace.

The story of Anne — nee Hyde, Countess of Ossory, given by Lord Dunboyne ties in with the information given by the spirit who contacted George. She was the daughter of Laurence, first Earl of Rochester, who was married to Henrietta, daughter of Richard, first Earl of Burlington. According to the Carte manuscripts after Anne's marriage to James Butler, Earl of Ossory at Burlington House in London on 20 July 1682, Lord Longford wrote to the Earl of Arran: 'The young bride is one of the prettiest ladies I ever saw and of a most excellent humour and my Lord and she are as fond of one another as you could wish'. She was mother of Lady Elizabeth Butler and, possibly Lady Mary Butler, who died as a child. Anne did, in fact, die after a miscarriage on 25 January 1685. She was buried, not where they looked in Kilkenny, but in Christ Church, Dublin. After her death her husband became the second Duke of Ormond on 21 July 1688.

In October 1919 Willie, George and baby Anne moved to No. 4 Broad Street in Oxford, England to avoid the war in Ireland. He wrote to Lady Gregory: 'It all seems very peaceful, with a green parrot on the landing and Anne staggering about full of destructiveness — they only heighten the sense of peace. If peace can ever come to this world again it should be here.'

The poet's sisters looked after Anne while Willie and George left for America where he gave a lecture tour. Also in America at that time was Eamonn de Valera, President of Ireland's new government. De Valera was trying to enlist support for Irish independence. Willie's friend Quinn brought him to hear De Valera speak in New York on 11 May 1920. Willie described him as: 'A living argument rather than a living man. All propaganda, no human life, but not bitter or hysterical or unjust . . . ' However, when he met him years later, he found in him a charm that did not come across in his speeches.

# 24

*Ah, but peace that comes at length,*
*Came when Time had touched her form.*

PEACE

While Willie was enjoying his new role as husband and
father he did not lose touch with Maud or events in
Ireland.

The Sinn Féin party ran for election in December 1918
with a policy of an Irish Republic with no connections
with Britain. The party was victorious. Dáil Éireann, the
new Irish parliament, met for the first time on 21 January
1919 with Eamonn de Valera as its first president. Maud's
friend, Arthur Griffith was appointed to a ministry, as was
his friend Michael Collins. Countess Markievicz was
nominated for the position of secretary of labour and so
became the first woman to be offered a cabinet ministry in
any Western European government. Maud was not considered for inclusion as she had been out of the country
for too long but her brother-in-law Joseph, took his place.
Joseph represented the old Fenian tradition, his hair snow
white after his jail experiences. When the roll was called a
large number of names drew the response 'imprisoned by
the foreign enemy' which would have delighted Maud.

Les Mouettes in Normandy had been sold and the proceeds used to buy a cottage in Glenmalure, County
Wicklow. At last Maud was in Ireland with her children
and the government she admired. In *Peace* Willie wrote:

*Ah, that Time could touch a form*
*That could show what Homer's age*
*Bred to be a hero's wage.*
*'Were not all her life but storm,*
*Would not painters paint a form*

114

*Of such noble lines,' I said,*
*'Such a delicate high head,*
*All that sternness amid charm,*
*All that sweetness amid strength?*
*Ah, but peace that comes at length,*
*Came when Time had touched her form.*

Maud and Iseult frequently visited AE's Sunday evenings held for artists and writers. A visitor to these evenings during the winter of 1918–19 was Francis Stuart, a seventeen year old aspiring poet from Antrim. He was a great admirer of Willie and was surprised to hear Maud and Iseult refer to him as 'poor Willie'. He was invited to their cottage in Wicklow and he and Iseult fell in love. He was eight years her junior and they belonged to different religions so they saw little hope of the families agreeing to marriage. In January 1920 they went to live together in a flat at Tottenham Court Road, London. During Maud's youth this type of relationship did not bother her but in her daughter's case she persuaded the pair to return to Dublin. Francis took instructions in the Catholic religion. He married Iseult in April 1920 and the couple lived with Maud.

Later that year Willie had trouble with his tonsils and came over to his friend Dr Oliver Gogarty to have them removed. Maud invited him to Wicklow where he wrote a poem to Ireland and Maud — 'I have loved you better than my soul for all my words . . . '

Iseult was pregnant at this time and, in January 1921, Francis went to London to sell a jewel that had been a wedding gift to Iseult from his family. He sent the money home but stayed on in London. A daughter, Dolores was born in March and the baby died in July. Although he shared her interest in Republican politics Maud's presence in the home was one reason for him not wanting to return.

115

Maud thought that she would help by taking, rather than sending, the couple to Europe but when this failed she appealed to her friend Willie for help. Willie had limited success.

She never left Willie alone for long. When a Mrs Desmond Fitzgerald asked for help to visit her husband at Arbour Hill military prison it was not to the authorities but to Willie that she turned for help and he gave it with great alacrity.

By July he was back in Oxford and Willie wrote again to Lady Gregory: 'It is a great joy to be back in this house again after many journeys and it looks very solemn and dignified to our eyes wearied by many irrelevant things...'

In August 1921 George and Willie had a son, Michael, and A. Norman Jeffares writes that in October Willie asked George to contact the Countess again to see if Michael was a reincarnation but could get no confirmation.

Of his children Willie wrote in *My Descendants*:

> *Having inherited a vigorous mind*
> *From my old fathers, I must nourish dreams*
> *And leave a woman and a man behind*
> *As vigorous of mind . . .*

According to an article in the *Irish Times*, 23 January 1989, Willie's 'old father' who had such an influence on his life was delighted with the news of his grandchildren. He spent the last eleven years of his life, happily painting a self-portrait commissioned by John Quinn. J.B. died in New York in 1922 and is buried in a country graveyard in the Adirondacks.

Lloyd George's government introduced ex-soldiers to keep order in Ireland. Called the Black and Tans the ex-soldiers caused havoc with assaults on life and property. Maud was instrumental in setting up the White Cross to help victims. Her son Seán became an active leader of an IRA squad at the age of sixteen and their home became a refuge for anyone on the run. Her housekeeper at the time was Kathleen Kearney, later to become mother of the playwright Brendan Behan.

In December 1921 a Treaty was signed between England and Ireland. This gave Ireland dominion status and Northern Ireland the right to opt out of the new state but it also required an oath of allegiance to the crown. De Valera, who had not travelled to England with the negotiating team, would not agree to the oath and resigned as president. Young Seán MacBride played an active part as a messenger between England and Ireland during the negotiation of the Treaty. A rift developed between the Free Staters who supported the Treaty and the Republicans who did not.

In a letter to the *Sunday Independent* on 3 February, 1974 Seán MacBride said: 'Mother was in favour of accepting the Treaty. She, not unnaturally, regarded it as a tremendous improvement on Home Rule and as a "stepping stone" to complete independence. She revised her views when the Four Courts were attacked and became strongly opposed to the Provisional Government.

'I opposed the acceptance of the Treaty on the grounds that it was an unacceptable compromise and that we could have obtained complete independence and unity by holding out a bit longer.'

Seán was in the Four Courts at the onset of the civil war, which may have hastened Maud's conversion. Francis Stuart, like Seán, supported the Republicans long before Maud did.

Because of their Republican sympathies, Maud's house was ransacked. The soldiers made a pile of her private papers, pictures, notebooks, letters including many from Willie. These were all burned in the centre of the road

117

outside her house. It is interesting to note that her treasured photographs of Lucien were saved from the disaster.

England approved the constitution of the Free State and special provision was made for the composition of an upper house of the senate. Thirty members were nominated representing aspects of Irish life and thirty were nominated by the Dáil.

In December 1922, while he was in London, Willie was nominated for the senate. According to Joseph Hone his friend Oliver St John Gogarty called to his house and wrote *Senator W.B. Yeats* on his letter box. Gogarty phoned George the following day to say that his election was due, not to his work for the Abbey but, to his membership of the IRB, which surprised George as it was the first time she had heard of Willie's connection with the organisation.

Willie accepted the honour and took his duties seriously. He was chairman of the committee which promoted Gaelic language, folklore and ancient poetry and was involved in selecting the animal designs for Irish coins. He also welcomed the salary of £360 per annum tax free.

Maud was disgusted with Willie because she said 'he became a senator of the Free State which voted flogging acts against young Republican soldiers still seeking to free Ireland from the contaminations of the British Empire.'

Willie enjoyed being a senator and dressed for the part. He continued until a bill was introduced to ban the introduction of divorce into Ireland, making an impassioned speech in favour of divorce as a right for the minority who were not Roman Catholic. Because it fell on deaf ears he did not seek re-election in 1928.

While he was a senator Maud was in trouble again with the government but would not ask Willie for help. Iseult did and Willie spoke to the then President, Cosgrave. Maud, in jail in Kilmainham, had gone on hunger-strike and Willie pleaded that while it would do Countess Markievicz no harm to remain in jail, Maud was delicate. Cosgrave remarked that women, doctors and clergy should keep out of politics as their business was with the sick. Maud, however, was released.

Seán like his mother, was imprisoned frequently, for his political beliefs. Iseult kept in contact with the Yeats family but Maud avoided Willie for ten years (because he had become a senator). She sorely missed his friendship but this void was filled in part by the companionship of Charlotte Despard, sister to Lord French. Charlotte became president and Maud secretary of the newly-formed Women's Prisoners Defence League and thereafter they became inseparable. They bought Roebuck House, Clonskeagh, jointly in 1922 with a view to setting up job-creation schemes in the house and extensive gardens. A jam-making company was one of their first enterprises.

That year Lady Gregory asked Willie to make a speech about the differences between the Free Staters and the Republicans but he declined saying: 'I feel that both sides are responsible for this whirlpool of hate.'

Honour followed honour for Willie. In July 1922, Belfast University gave him an honourary degree and this was followed in December by a doctorate in Letters from Dublin University. According to Jeffares one day in 1923 the editor of the *Irish Times* phoned to tell him that he had been awarded the Nobel Prize for Literature. Willie's first question was how much money would be given with the award. The £7,500, a vast sum in those days, gave him a new financial standing. He and George were delighted with the news yet could not find a bottle of wine in the house so they cooked sausages instead to celebrate. The following evening he hosted a dinner party at the Shelbourne Hotel and was delighted when his first telegram of congratulations arrived from James Joyce.

The presentations of the Diploma and Medal were made in the hall of the Swedish Academy on 10 December. Willie spoke about the Irish theatre in the Academy and paid tribute to Lady Gregory and John Synge. In later years he was flattered to hear the Royal family 'liked him better than any previous Nobel Prize winner as he had the manners of a courtier.'

# 25

*Vague memories, nothing but memories,*
*But in the grave, all, all shall be renewed . . .*
BROKEN DREAMS

The Yeats family did not escape involvement in the terrible civil war. Both sides visited them at Ballylee. The Republicans came to blow up the bridge leading into the tower. Willie asked if he might bring the children to safety. He was refused so they sought safety in an upper room.

In the years that Maud avoided Willie he enjoyed life as the 'public smiling man' and also as husband and father. George turned a blind eye to his occasional affairs.

In letters to John Quinn Willie described the home scene: 'It is a great pleasure to live in a place where George makes, at every moment, a fourteenth-century picture. And out of doors, with the hawthorn all in blossom, all along the river banks, everything is so beautiful that to go elsewhere is to leave beauty behind.'

Of his children he wrote' . . . your godson has eight teeth and nothing ails Anne but her theology. When she says the Lord's Prayer she makes such interjections as "Father not in heaven — father in the study".'

In the winter of 1931–32 Lady Gregory's health was failing rapidly. Willie visited her regularly at Coole and he and AE discussed the founding of an Academy of Letters to promote the intellectual and poetic quality of Irish life.

February 1932 brought the Fianna Fáil party into power with De Valera at the head. It had a mandate to remove the vote of allegiance to the British crown. Willie had no objection to this but when they hinted at introducing censorship at the Abbey he looked for an interview with De Valera. Willie wrote to a friend: 'I was impressed by his simplicity and honesty though we differed throughout. It was a curious experience, each recognising the other's point of view completely. I had gone there full of suspicion, but my suspicion vanished at once . . . '

When Lady Gregory died on 18 September, 1932 Willie's loss was incalculable. She had been such an important part of his life that it was hard to imagine life without her. With her death his links with the west of Ireland were broken and he and George looked for a house in Dublin. Their new home, Riversdale, was about a mile beyond Rathfarnham and had views of the mountains and the bay. The gardens were well kept and the small house had ample room for Willie's books and some of Jack's paintings.

Shortly after the house move Willie went on a tour of America to raise money for the proposed Academy of Letters. When he came back Maud contacted him to express her approval of the Academy. Willie's son, Michael carried messages between Roebuck House and Riversdale. It was some years now since Willie had written in *Broken Dreams*:

> *There is grey in your hair.*
> *Young men no longer suddenly catch their breath*
> *When you are passing . . .*

> *A young man when the old are done talking*
> *Will say to an old man, 'Tell me of that lady*
> *The poet, stubborn with his passion sang us*
> *When age might well have chilled his blood.'*

> *Vague memories, nothing but memories,*
> *But in the grave, all, all shall be renewed.*
> *The certainty that I shall see that lady*
> *Leaning or standing or walking*
> *In the first loveliness of womanhood,*

*And with the fervour of my youthful eyes,*
*Has set me muttering like a fool . . .*

Maud's approval of the Academy and the messages that passed between them did much to heal the longstanding rift. He asked if she would meet him once more and suggested the Kildare Street Club in Dublin as a venue. This turned out to be a bad choice as ladies were barred from the main rooms and they were confined to the hall where a portrait of a viceroy reminded Maud of British rule in Ireland. Willie added fuel to the fire by introducing her to an Anglo-Irish peer. She felt that this flaunted his association with the British and left.

A bronzed plaster bust of Maud, the work of a young sculptor Lawrence Campbell, inspired Willie's final poem about Maud.

In *A Bronze Head* he compares her appearance then with that of her youth:

> *No dark-tomb haunter once; her form all full*
> *As though with magnanimity of light,*
> *Yet a most gentle woman; who can tell*
> *Which of her forms has shown her substance right?*
> *Or maybe substance can be composite : . .*
> *Or else I thought her supernatural;*
> *As though a sterner eye looked through her eye*
> *On this foul world in its decline and fall . . .*

He continued to write but his health failed. With his devoted George he divided his time between Ireland England and France. His later poems were published by Cuala Press in April 1938 under the title *New Poems*.

That year Maud was writing her autobiography *A Servant of the Queen* — the title of which was a reference to Queen Maeve. She asked his permission to quote him and he replied: 'Yes of course you can say what you like about me. I have never felt the Irish struggle "hopeless". Let it be "exhausting struggle" or "tragic struggle" or some such phrase. I wanted the struggle to go on but in a different way. You can, of course quote those poems of mine, but if you do not want my curse, do not misprint them. People constantly misprint quotations . . . '

The Abbey put on his play *Purgatory* in August 1938 and he made his last public appearance at the first night of the play.

# 26

*Murmur a little sadly, how love fled
And paced upon the mountains overhead . . .*
WHEN YOU ARE OLD

In their twilight years Maud and Willie did not meet very frequently. She felt the partitioning of Ireland was an important issue while he would not agree. This political difference was put aside in the late summer of 1938 when she called to Riversdale to visit him for the last time. He had become very feeble and had difficulty in rising to his feet. Both in their seventies they talked of times past and, when she was about to leave, he said that they should have continued with their Castle of Heroes. Taken by surprise that he should have remembered this Maud could find no words to reply.

Some weeks later Willie read in a newspaper report that part of a letter, signed by Maud was found on an IRA suspect. Impressed he commented 'What a woman! What vitality! What energy'. He wrote to a friend, Sir William Rothenstein and asked if someone might draw her portrait. 'No artist had ever drawn her, and just now she looks magnificent.' His wish was not fulfilled at that time.

He left with George for England and then the Riviera. He stayed at the Hotel Ideal Sejour at Cap Martin where Michael joined them for Christmas. On 4 January Willie wrote to Lady Elizabeth Pelham: 'I have put away everything that can be put away that I may speak what I have to speak . . . I am happy, and I think full of energy, of an energy I had despaired of. It seems to me that I have found what I wanted . . .'

He died at 2pm on Saturday 28 January 1939 and his body was taken to Roquebrune, overlooking Cap Martin and Monaco. His grave there was a temporary resting place with a plain stone which read *W.B. Yeats 1865–1939.*

After Willie's death, George collected up old letters that Maud had written to Willie and sent them to her. This delighted Maud as most of Willie's letters had been burned when her house was raided.

Seán continued his involvement with the IRA. He had qualified in law and when De Valera's government brought charges against some of its members Seán defended them in court.

He started a new political party Clann na Poblachta. Maud stood for election but was not successful. In 1947 Seán's party took office as part of a Coalition Government and he became minister for external affairs. Maud must have been pleased when this government finally declared Ireland a Republic and withdrew from the British Commonwealth. She would have preferred if it had been for the entire thirty-two counties.

In September 1948, Seán, as minister for external affairs, welcomed Willie's body to its final resting-place in Drumcliff graveyard 'under Bare Ben Bulben's head' in his beloved Sligo.

In *Under Ben Bulben* Willie had written his own epitaph

> *No marble, no conventional phrase;*
> *On limestone quarried near the spot*
> *By his command these words are cut:*
> *'Cast a cold eye*
> *On life, on death.*
> *Horseman, pass by!'*

Maud lived on for many years after Willie's death, a well-known figure in widow's weeds. In her old age she must have read and re-read the poem Willie wrote for her when they were still young. *When You are Old* is based on a sonnet by Ronsard to his mistress: